People in Pain

BOOKS BY WAYNE E. OATES
Published by The Westminster Press

The Struggle to Be Free:
  My Story and Your Story

The Christian Pastor
  Third Edition, Revised

Your Particular Grief

The Religious Care
  of the Psychiatric Patient

Pastoral Counseling

When Religion Gets Sick

On Becoming Children of God

Pastoral Counseling in Social Problems:
  Extremism, Race, Sex, Divorce

Protestant Pastoral Counseling

The Revelation of God in Human Suffering

Anxiety in Christian Experience

The Bible in Pastoral Care

Potentials: Guides for Productive Living
  Books 1-11, edited by Wayne E. Oates
  Convictions That Give You Confidence
  Your Right to Rest

Christian Care Books
  Books 1-12, edited by Wayne E. Oates
  Pastor's Handbook, Vols. I and II

WITH CHARLES E. OATES

People in Pain: Guidelines for Pastoral Care

WITH KIRK H. NEELY

Where to Go for Help
(Revised and Enlarged Edition)

People in Pain
Guidelines for Pastoral Care

Wayne E. Oates
and Charles E. Oates, M.D.

The Westminster Press
Philadelphia

Book design by Gene Harris

First edition

Published by The Westminster Press®
Philadelphia, Pennsylvania

PRINTED IN THE UNITED STATES OF AMERICA

9 8 7 6 5 4 3 2 1

Library of Congress Cataloging in Publication Data

Oates, Wayne Edward, 1917–
  People in pain.

  Bibliography: p.
  Includes index.
  1. Pain—Religious aspects—Christianity.
2. Pastoral medicine. 3. Pain. I. Oates, Charles E.,
1953–   . II. Title.
BT732.7.063 1985   259'.4   85-5403
ISBN 0-664-24674-5 (pbk.)

To
Diane

Contents

Acknowledgments

We are especially indebted to Mrs. Jenni Khaliel, for her expert and invaluable research assistance in our study of the problems of pain and pain management and for her careful preparation of the manuscript.

We owe a debt of gratitude to innumerable persons who have been both our patients and our teachers concerning their private worlds of pain. Their discoveries and wisdom show anonymously but eloquently through these pages.

We appreciate beyond words the companionship, participation, and sacrifices of Pauline Rhodes Oates and Diane Marie Oates, our beloved wives. Their wisdom and tender love have sustained us.

Wayne E. Oates, Ph.D.
School of Medicine
University of Louisville
Louisville, Kentucky

Charles E. Oates, M.D.
Rush-Presbyterian-St. Luke's Medical Center
Chicago, Illinois

1

The Experience of Pain
in the Presence of God

As a pastor, you suggest the reality of God to people you meet. You do this without saying so when those you meet know you to be a pastor. Some of these people, far more of them than tell us, are in pain. They are often bed patients, at home, in a hospital, or in a nursing home. But not all of them are bedridden. Some can move around but live on one kind of disability payment or another. Others —many of them—are carrying on their daily work *and* bearing pain too.

Some of these people, wherever they are, talk with you about their pain. Some talk about little else *but* their pain. Others who are in pain may never—or rarely—mention it. All of them, however, would agree that their pain is not some vague suffering, or evil, but a specific and extremely unpleasant feeling associated with one or more parts of the body. In brief, when they tell you that they "hurt," they are not speaking metaphorically. It is the real thing—physical pain!

Pain of this specific kind—not evil in general, suffering in general —is what this book is about. As authors, we have chosen to collaborate with each other as minister and physician in order to help you as pastor with your understanding of people in acute and chronic pain and with your care of these people. We are particularly concerned about the pain patient's perception of himself or herself as a spiritual being existing in pain before God and in relation to God. We think of God as God is known through Jesus Christ and as experienced by contemporary Christians. We know that, because Jesus of Nazareth and most of his followers in his time on earth were Jewish, the Christian message of today must include the prophetic heritage of Judaism. Although we speak from a Christian world view, we do not exclude from our discussion rabbis or any others who minister to people in pain. Buddhists and Hindus have much to teach us about the disciplines of pain control and management. Their experience in direct spiritual management of pain is finally being assimilated into Western science and religion in a creative way, and we affirm that contribution here.

The very nature of our collaboration emphasizes our commendation of the factual data offered by the medical profession for understanding and caring for patients with either acute or chronic pain. The wisdom of the body is constantly being searched out by physicians. Pain is one messenger of that wisdom, but not the only one. In this book, we consider these messages to be written for our instruction in the tissue and the biochemistry of the body. We are convinced that your having this translation of medical teachings about pain will equip you to observe, listen, and respond to people in pain more knowledgeably and empathically.

Our intention is to set the measure of present-day knowledge of pain states in the context of the total person's spiritual pilgrimage with God and with the significant humans in his or her life. For this reason, our first topic of discussion is the experience of pain in the presence of God.

What Is Pain?

One of the most frequent definitions of pain is that it is "an unpleasant experience which we primarily associate with tissue damage or describe in terms of tissue damage or both" (Merskey and Spear, p. 21).* Physicians have more specific definitions of pain, which amount to descriptions of the process. They speak first of *nociceptors* (nerve endings that are stimulated by injury). This injury leads to "pain sensation, suffering, and behavioral response [that] is the net effect of incredibly complex interactions of ascending and descending neural systems, biochemical, physiological, and psychological mechanisms and neocortical processes" (Ng and Bonica, p. 3).

As a pastor, however, you may seek a biblical definition. Pain is described in Genesis as punishment in childbirth for Eve because of yielding to temptation in the Garden of Eden. Even today we speak of "labor pains" with reference to childbirth. However, in Romans 8:22–23, Paul uses a more redemptive metaphor of pain in childbirth to describe our eager anticipation of becoming children of God and our receiving the "redemption of our bodies." In the Genesis account, Adam's work is similarly cursed; both linguistically

---

*The full reference for this work, and others similarly cited, is in the Bibliography.

and psychologically, pain has been historically associated with work, toil, and the "sweat of our face." Yet in more redeemed perceptions of work we perceive it not as pain but as the calling of God. As Jesus said in John 9:4, "We must work the works of him who sent me, while it is day; night comes, when no one can work."

Nevertheless, pain is associated with punishment in the New Testament also. In Revelation 16:10–11, "men gnawed their tongues in anguish and cursed the God of heaven for their pain and sores, and they did not repent of their deeds." A similar abandonment to pain and anguish is found in Isaiah 65:14. In stark contrast to this abandonment and curse by God in the experience of pain, Isaiah 53:10–11 speaks of the pain of the Suffering Servant as being an "offering for sin," which the Lord wills to prosper, and promises that the Suffering Servant shall see the pain or "travail of his soul and be satisfied." Redemption from pain triumphs in the New Testament, nevertheless. In Revelation 21:3–4, the New Jerusalem is described:

> Behold, the dwelling of God is with men. He will dwell with them, and they shall be his people, and God himself will be with them; he will wipe away every tear from their eyes, and death shall be no more, neither shall there be mourning nor crying nor pain any more, for the former things have passed away.

Pain in the biblical perspective is real; it can be both destructive and redemptive, debilitating and creative. Pain may produce a feeling of the absence of God or an invitation of the presence of God. Martin Marty speaks of the cry of the absence of God which "can also come . . . to a waste space left when the divine is distant, the sacred is remote, when God is silent" (p. 2). Some pain patients will assert that the self-absorption caused by persistent pain does indeed make prayer difficult and God remote to them. Yet the same person who insists on "centering upon God" will assert also that, as Martin Marty goes on to say, "a wintry sort of spirituality also produces occasions when the Absence leaves the horizon and the Presence realizes itself. 'The Lord is close to those whose courage is broken and he saves those whose spirit is crushed (Psalm 34:18).' "

Pastors and physicians alike are debtors not only to a Hebrew biblical heritage but also to a Greek philosophical heritage for our understanding of what pain is. The biblical word *ponos* for pain also appears in both classical Greek and biblical Koiné Greek. Homer, in the ninth century B.C., spoke of pain as a "toil of war"; that is, combat pain. Even in this century, John Bonica, the pioneer in pain research who established the first interdisciplinary pain clinic at the

University of Washington in Seattle, began his lifelong study of pain with combat casualties among World War II veterans.

Hesiod, in the eighth century B.C., defined pain in terms of exercises, bodily exertion, and fatigue. Even today, exercise is both a cause of pain and a source for the relief of pain, especially muscle spasms. But it was not until the fifth century B.C. that Hippocrates undertook a scientific diagnosis of the different causes of pain and a scientific search for specific ways to relieve it. About the same time, Herodotus expanded the meaning of the word "pain" to include any kind of punishment, trouble, stress, or suffering.

The merging of pain with punishment pervades history. The Genesis story of the fall of humankind gives pain as the punishment for wrongdoing. The Latin words used for pain are *dolor, cruciare,* and *angere* (meaning "mental and physical pain," "to torture," and "to cause suffocation or anguish," respectively). One of these terms, *cruciare,* captures the punishment dimension of pain and is one of the words from which we get "crucify." (*Crucifigere* is the other.) The French word for pain, *peine,* is also the word for punishment and penalty.

Therefore, from a pastoral point of view, when a patient asks you, "What have I done to deserve this pain?" he or she expresses a view of pain that has been in the mind of the human race for centuries. The religiously devout person may say, "Why does God let this happen?" The secular-minded person may ask, "Why was I so stupid as to let this happen to me?" The fatalist will say, "The odds are against me!" The underlying feeling for all is, "For some reason I am being punished." This is the nonrational, primitive definition of pain in the deeper levels of consciousness of the pain-ridden population.

Some Religious Attitudes Toward Pain

The discussion of the underlying, underived association of pain with punishment suggests that many other attitudes and responses to pain grow in the patient's mind as he or she attempts to pray or perceives himself or herself as being in the presence or absence of God. Some of these attitudes can be readily identified: denial, stoicism, magical thinking, realism. Doing so may enable a pastor more quickly to become empathetic within the private world, or *Eigenwelt,* of the patient.

Denial. Next to the pervasiveness of the attitude that all pain is punishment, religious denial of the reality of pain seems to be most common. In everyday marketplace and bedside conversation, denial surfaces in such remarks as:

"If I had faith enough, I wouldn't be hurting this way."

"A *good* Christian wouldn't complain as much as I do."

"I wish I could have the kind of trust in Jesus that —— has; I would not have this pain."

"If you only would let the Holy Spirit take possession of you, you wouldn't have this pain!"

"You must have some unrecognized spiritual problem; if you could see it and work through it in prayer, your pain would leave you."

Denial takes an institutional form in Christian Science teachings, although many of these practices of thought and behavior control do indeed favorably affect the perception of pain. Similarly, the hypnotic effect of many Pentecostal believers may relieve hysterical, psychogenic pain that has muscular tension and stress at its base. Hypnosis—quite apart from religious considerations—is a useful means of alleviating pain, particularly chronic pain. It "(1) enables the patient to alter his perception of pain, thus gaining a greater mastery of his body; (2) it diminishes anxiety and depression; and (3) it enables the patient to become more functional and less dependent on others. Especially is lowering of dependency on family members helpful" (Mutter and Karnilow, p. 1098). However, when the dependence is shifted to a practitioner, as in the case of some preachers or religious groups, ethical issues arise. Is the hypnotic or placebo factor frankly stated? Is it an open and above-board part of the covenant that this *is* hypnosis? Is the hypnotist personally prepared to stay by and follow through with the patient over the long pull of time? The absence of an open understanding that this *is* hypnotism, albeit a *means* that can indeed be blessed by God, leads to manipulation and the promise of a panacea that could leave the patient in a state worse than the first.

Denial has a long history. It is rooted in neo-Platonic teachings about the unreality, unimportance, and even evil of the human body. The Christian version of this is found in the Monarchianism of Theodotus (A.D. 190). His description of the Christ, whom he carefully separated from Jesus, goes like this:

Christ came into existence in some such way as this: that Jesus is, indeed, a man born of a virgin according to the counsel of the Father

—living in common with all men, and most pious by birth; and that afterward at his baptism in the Jordan, the Christ from above, having descended in the form of a dove, entered into him; wherefore miraculous powers were not exerted by him before the Spirit, which he says is Christ, having descended, was manifested in him. Some think that he did not become God until the descent of the Spirit; others, until after his resurrection from the dead (Seeberg, pp. 163, 166–167).

You will readily recognize Theodotus's teaching as a continuation of the Gnostic teaching that the Fourth Gospel and the First Letter of John denounced as spurious. The Fourth Gospel insists that the Word became flesh (John 1:14), and 1 John 4:2–3 says, "By this you know the Spirit of God: every spirit which confesses that Jesus Christ has come in the flesh is of God, and every spirit which does not confess Jesus is not of God. This is the spirit of antichrist, of which you heard that it was coming, and now it is in the world already." The reality of the human body cannot be denied. Its pain is real. *Through* Jesus Christ's body and *through* our own bodies God is revealed to us, not in spite of the body.

Stoicism. A second attitude toward pain is stoicism. Here a person's attitude goes in the opposite direction from denial. To the stoic, pain and the body that expresses it are real as can be. Whatever pain is present is the patient's lot. It is our duty to conform to whatever our destiny may be, a part of which is pain. The wise person, then, endures pain free from passion, unsubdued by its grief, and submissive to natural law. Does this sound familiar? Both the pain patient and the physician—without conscious stoicism—often convey these attitudes. Much Christian pietism that says "It's the Lord's will" expresses this essentially stoical stance toward life.

Secular-thinking persons will express stoical attitudes in terms of the statistical odds or probabilities gained from medical studies of people with their specific pain syndrome. The particular religious form that counting the odds statistically takes is "hoping for the best and preparing for the worst." Acute cancer pain and cardiac pain prompt this kind of attitude more than chronic pain such as arthritic and low back pain. The eagerness of chronic pain patients to pin hopes on one surgical procedure after another temporarily pushes them into calculating the statistical success and failure rate of each new operation.

More often than not, however, the stoical attitude of a pain patient takes these forms in pastoral interviews:

"The Lord will not put more on me than I can bear."

"If I were a stronger person, I would not let this pain get to me."

"The doctor told me I could take the pain medicine every four hours, but by the Lord's help I just take it once a day."

"I keep praying to be able to eat this pain."

"I just grin and bear it, by God!"

"Nobody can help me. It's just me and the pain fighting it out with each other."

Magical Thinking. A third attitude, which may be considered a strange blend of denial and stoicism, is magical thinking. Such thinking is pre-logical, archaic, and childishly concrete in nature. The pain patient who thinks magically assumes that he or she is an exception and should not have pain of any kind. He or she looks for a "special" person who will work a "special" miracle never done before or possible later. The form this takes in pastoral conversation is: "Why would God let this happen to me? I know God has led me to this doctor, who is going to take away this pain. They have never seen a case like mine, but this doctor is sure I can be made well!"

More often, however, expectation of a magical cure takes the form of rejecting doctors and relying on the special curative powers of a chosen religious personality, an exorcist, an evangelist, a particular radio or television preacher, or even a medium, someone who claims to be able to get in touch with the dead. The magician controls supernatural forces through ritual, spell, séance, sleight of hand, and incantation. The pain patient who has little or no perception of the relation between simple cause and effect, to say nothing of a systems or field approach to many interacting causes and effects, is highly susceptible to magical approaches—to religion and pain relief alike. Pain patients who are also suffering from various psychiatric disorders at the same time are concrete and magical in their thinking, confusing cause and effect in their experience of pain. This is not to say, however, that persons who resort to magical cures are necessarily mentally ill.

Realism. The attitudes of denial, stoicism, and magic appear in most pain patients' thoughts and conversations at different times

and places. Reality, when presented as pain, particularly when the
end is not in sight, is a harsh taskmaster. However, a realistic attitude, particularly in the absence or presence of God, is a way of
dealing constructively with pain. In a sense, this is what this whole
book is about. Nevertheless, some specific dimensions of realism in
dealing with pain can be described here and developed more fully
as we move to the more detailed inquiry.

The realistic attitude toward pain is characterized by a frank acceptance of pain as a part of our creatureliness, finitude, and frailty.
Pain is both a bane and a blessing of being human. It is always a bane
in that it is uncomfortable, unpleasant, and distracting. It is always
a blessing in that it lets us know that something is wrong with our
body that calls for attention. Even the chronic pain patient learns
to recognize "new" pain, register alarm about it, and seek diagnosis
and treatment for it separately from "old" pain that is ordinarily
there.

The recognition of frailty and weakness is, in a sense, a gift. Pain
patients have a reminder of it ever before them. People without pain
regularly assume that there are *no* limits to what they can do, to how
many hours they can go without sleep, to how many responsibilities
they can take on. They may even boast of never knowing what it is
to be tired. In this sense, the pain-free person entertains the illusion
that he or she is special, an exception, with no limits. Pain is a distant
early warning system in the realistic management of stress and in
the necessity for rest, renewal, and re-creation. We are creatures,
but divine Providence has given us the privilege and responsibility
of continually re-creating our own lives. Thus God's strength is
perfected in our limitations and weaknesses.

This leads to the second dimension of a realistic attitude toward
pain. We have been created not only with limitations but also with
intelligence. We not only feel pain; we also perceive pain. The mind
of humankind is the candle of the Lord. With the effective use of
intelligence, pain can be outwitted. Our capacity to *perceive* pain is
powerful (see Arnold). Having an *accurate* perception is the rub!
Hence, in a realistic attitude toward pain, a person acts responsibly
to build a true-to-fact perception of his or her pain and to build a
wise way of life on the basis of this perception. This means that he
or she studies not only what the pain is caused by but also what it
causes him or her to think and do. Before God, the person takes
responsibility for being a partner with God, family, pastor, physician, and intimate friends in constructive management of the pain.
This is a consecration of our total body and mind to God in a very

specific way. Thus, responses to pain in word and behavior become a form of meditation and prayer in fellowship with God and one's family, physician, and pastor and the spiritual community more generally.

The Christian has a fellow participant in pain in Jesus Christ. The scriptures tell us that "although he was a Son, he learned obedience through what he suffered" (Heb. 5:8). The pain he experienced was acute, demanding massive tolerance as he suffered death on the cross. Psychologist David Bakan points (p. 67) to "the great significance of the Cross as a symbol of the meaning of pain, a symbol through which large segments of humanity might be joined together. . . . Indeed, one might well argue that one of the major psychological uses of Christianity has been to overcome the essential loneliness and privacy of pain." Jesus Christ is our fellow pilgrim in whatever pain we bear. We are not alone. Christ calls the Christian from the isolation and self-absorption that pain induces into community with others who are in pain and need help and in comradeship with physicians, physiotherapists, ministers, and the corporate fellowship of prayer.

The end result of this realism is an ordering and discipline of life as a whole that is more than the stoical hardening of oneself in isolation to pain. In the words of the Okinawan proverb:

> Pain makes you think,
> Thought makes you wise,
> Wisdom makes pain bearable.

Such wisdom suggests that the pain patient is an informed patient who is teachable by physicians and others. Therefore, the informed patient insists on such teaching. He or she complies with therapeutic instructions as a form of prayer and is answerable to physicians for the careful use of medications and for disciplines such as weight control, smoking, drinking, and prescribed physical activity.

Pastoral Awareness of Pain Patients' Needs

As a pastor you see pain patients often—in the home, at church, in the hospital. George Patterson, a professor of religion and medicine at the University of Iowa, says (p. 10), "In considering the emotional and spiritual needs of persons in pain, it is helpful to distinguish between three types of pain—acute, chronic, and terminal—each of which may require a somewhat different approach." The need for an end to pain emerges in quite different qualities of hope and hopelessness. If you as a pastor perceive your task as a generator of hope and an opponent of hopelessness, you have a major challenge when caring for all kinds of pain patients.

In the second place, pain is not all bad; its presence invariably raises the issues of meaning, purpose, and vocation in life. The disability of pain patients from their work alone is difficult to overestimate. The profound question of *quo vadis?*— where is the person going?—is a distinct vocational concern for pastors who represent the "glory of God in the Christian calling." Hence, throughout this book, the person's sense of meaning, purpose, calling, and vocation in the absence and presence of God will be of major importance. We will struggle with the ambiguity of pain and pleasure, as Paul Tillich does when he says (1976, p. 56):

> The ambiguity of pain and pleasure is most conspicuous in a phenomenon which is often called morbid but which is universally present in healthy as well as sick life—the experience of pain in pleasure and of pleasure in pain. The psychological material substantiating this ambiguity in the self-creation of life is extensive but not fully understood. In itself it is not a matter of an unambiguous distortion of life—as the term morbid would indicate—but rather an everpresent symptom of the ambiguity of life under the dimension of self-awareness.

We have our work cut out for us! In the next chapter, we will consider pastoral encounters with pain sufferers. Then we will turn to medical descriptions of pain.

2

Pastoral Encounters
with Pain Sufferers

When people present to you, as a pastor, their dilemmas in managing pain, they rarely do so in the earliest stages of this experience. They more often come to your study or counseling room as a last resort. Many times they do not come to you on their own initiative. You meet them in your regular rounds of hospital visitation. Quite often, they will recite to you a litany of the numerous things they have tried to relieve the pain. They may have been to many different doctors, with little or no success in ending their suffering. They may have been operated on many times without relief. In many instances, they have had surgery repeatedly at the same location in their body. They may report that after the surgeries they are worse off, perhaps because of the buildup of scar tissue. Yet this is not the case with all persons who have had such surgeries. Even luckless patients will report having gone to a given surgeon because a friend of theirs had done so and gotten excellent results —"never had any more trouble." But they, *they* were different; the pain continued or got worse.

Furthermore, some of the people whom you visit or who visit you may depend heavily on one or more of a variety of drugs. They may think of themselves as hooked on this or that medication. Others may recount having been to other ministers, to faith healers, exorcists, or television evangelists, and they may expect magic from you.

One refrain that will be heard often is: "Everybody tells me there is nothing wrong with me. They tell me it is all in my mind." They come to you in a mixture of desperation and hope—desperation when they are not believed when they say they are in pain; hope that you will offer them some as yet untried avenue of relief.

You are immediately struck by their helplessness, and their story leaves you feeling helpless. You ask yourself, "What on earth can I do? What really can I mean to this person? What should I know in order both to do and be what is most needed of me?" These are questions to which this book is addressed, because we are convinced that you are a vital part of the healing team and the caring community of the pain patients whom you meet.

Any member of a responsive team of those who combine efforts to bring relief and hope to pain patients needs information, wisdom, and the capacity to take the patients' complaints seriously. The first complaint pastors are apt to make snap judgments about is the one that no one believes them but thinks that all problems are in their minds. To climb this mountainous question and be honestly and faithfully related to the patient, let us review some of the data on the issue of "psychogenic" or psychologically based pain.

The Credibility of the Patient's Report

Pain, as George Engel and Thomas Szasz say (p. 900), "falls into the category of private data—experience which cannot be simultaneously shared and reported by any one other than the person experiencing it." Therefore, to say that the pain is "all in your mind," or even that it is psychologically caused, is often interpreted by patients as an insult to their credibility. "You think I am putting on and putting you on when I say that I hurt" is often their reaction, whether verbal or nonverbal. Another interpretation is that you think they are crazy. Their self-esteem is at stake. Furthermore, they may assume that you think their pain is not real if you think it is psychologically based.

The fallacy underlying this bad miscommunication is the old mind–body dualism in the thinking of both scientists and lay people. A far better approach is to express full confidence that when the patient thinks and says he or she hurts, that patient indeed hurts, as far as you are concerned. You may say that many sources of pain do not show up on x-ray and in other laboratory tests. Your forthright assurance could go something like this: "You hurt. You are having trouble making it clear to people who are treating you just what your pain is like. When you tell me that you hurt, I believe you. I want you to feel that I am taking you seriously. You might wonder what are some of the things that can cause pain that don't show up on x-rays and laboratory tests. We can find out." In other words, you give assurance and stimulate curiosity.

Stress as a Source of Pain

A person can much more readily accept the idea that stress is a source of pain than such interpretations as "It is all in your mind." As we shall see later, stress can be both physiological and psychological. For example, muscle spasm can be caused by stress and cause pain at the same time. Acute pain itself is a stressor. Stress contributes to the pain and reinforces brain activity associated with pain. The substances that transmit nerve impulses are increased during stress situations. "Stress and pain mutually reenforce each other. Stress itself, whether organic or emotional, can modify pain" (Soulairac, p. 75). One of the important factors in the amount of cerebral response to pain is the degree of control an animal or person can exert over the stressor. The intimate intertwining of the emotional and physical dimensions of the pain experience is demonstrable at the laboratory level of stress experiments.

Therefore, one of the specific concerns you as a pastor can address is the number of psychological and social pressures the person is having to bear in addition to the pain itself. What strains and burdens are being carried? George Engel lists some burdens he identified in the lives of pain-prone patients whom he treated. Many of these are common topics of a pastoral conversation, whether persons ever mention pain to you or not:

A severe loss or threatened loss, which may be the loss of a loved one, the loss of a job, the loss of favor in the eyes of those whose approval one values

A history of having been abused or molested

A severe burden of conscious or unconscious guilt or shame

A load of unexpressed and unfulfilled aggression, including unresolved angers and running battles with other people

A history of suffering and defeat and intolerance of success, often resulting in a large number of painful injuries, operations, and treatments

Identification, conscious or unconscious, with an important person who has also suffered much pain

Engel mentions other stressful conditions and relationships, but these are the common, everyday stresses that people usually present to their pastor. You therefore learn quickly to listen carefully to all that a pain patient is saying and not just to the pain talk.

If you perceive yourself as a spiritual director in people's lives, these concerns are of primary spiritual importance to you as you minister to the pain-prone person. You have no major commitment to remove the symptoms of pain about which the person complains and despairs. However, the losses, feelings of having been abused, fears of failure or success, and others listed are primary concerns for any spiritual director.

Sometimes pain patients will themselves relate their pain directly to the burdens they are unloading in conversation with you. At other times, they report that their very act of discussing their stresses has lessened the amount of pain they feel, enabled them to sleep better at night, and given them an increased sense of hope and fresh energy for getting on with life. For this you can all give thanks to God. Be hesitant to assume that you yourself created this result. Relief from pain can be a good side effect of effective pastoral work. To *promise* it as a skill of your own puts you in the position of relieving the patient of responsibility. You can in your own quiet way actually *do* something about the pain state without creating false hopes and promises. There are patterns of pain management that actually reduce and at times remove pain. But they, themselves, are their own priest before God. At any time, they can confess their burdens to God. They can accept disciplines that will yield more lasting results in their struggle with pain.

Thus, to accept responsibility as a spiritual director in enabling patients to unload some of their stresses and make wise decisions as to what to do about them by the help of God is a primary goal of your pastoral work. This work may be left undone by other persons treating the pain, who may or may not see this task as within their area of expertise or concern.

Behavioral and Psychiatric Disorders Related to Pain

As a spiritual director, you are not naive. You have both the wisdom of the serpent and the harmlessness of the dove. Pain patients can indeed be consciously deceptive or emotionally ill, with pain as the focus of either the deception or the emotional illness or both.

Malingering. One common behavioral disorder is malingering, which is the willful, deliberate, and fraudulent feigning or exaggeration of the symptoms of illness or injury for the purpose of achieving a desired end. One such end would be to get out of work responsibilities—at school, on a job, or in the home. Another would be to collect money for injuries supposedly sustained in an automobile or a work-related accident. A malingerer might tell you about all this so that you might appear as a character witness in a court proceeding. This kind of behavior occurs often enough that pain clinics in university settings do not accept patients for assessment and treatment if legal actions are in process. They ask the person to wait to seek help until these have been settled. As a pastor, you should know from your previous knowledge of the character of the person whether you are being taken in and used. Ordinarily, a pastor is wise to stay out of litigation as much as possible.

Pain Complaints in Psychiatric Illnesses. Several psychiatric conditions involve pain complaints of patients. The most common is probably *somatization disorder,* in which more or less unconscious emotional problems are converted into physical complaints. For example, the person who has a self-concept of being totally self-sufficient may develop an intense esophageal muscle spasm when someone important to them leaves, even for a journey, to say nothing of abandonment, divorce, or death. This spasm is very painful and mimics a heart attack. Another example is the hypochondriac who may be preoccupied with having a serious disease such as cancer even though careful diagnosis demonstrates that this is not the case. Even so, the unrealistic fear or belief of having the disease persists, despite medical reassurance, and causes the person to be unable to function in the family, at work, or in social groupings. Still another example of psychiatric disorders in which pain is an associated feature is depression. Fuller discussions of both anxiety and depression will appear in chapter 6. Suffice it to say that these persons are not malingering and they are not intentionally deceiving you. Their suffering is intense and needs to be taken seriously. You are fortunate indeed if such patients are already being seen by a physician who is a specialist in internal medicine and whom you have permission to consult.

The Disability Factor

Of intense pastoral concern is the degree to which the pain suffered renders the person incapable of doing regular work or causes the person to lose confidence in the ability to do regular work. Lurking in this issue is the persistent question as to whether the person's dislike for, disenchantment with, or positive desire to ma-

linger preceded and contributed to the pain syndrome or whether
the pain itself eroded the person's ability and confidence as a working member of society.

"In the United States alone, about 90 million people suffer from
chronic pain, including the pain of low back ailments, arthritis,
headaches, and cancer . . . [and that] pain accounts for 750 million
lost work days a year and costs Americans at least $65 billion annu-
ally," according to Carol Fletcher (p. 3236). In computing costs
reported in surveys on back pain, headaches, and arthritis, L. K. Ng
and John Bonica estimate that the costs of chronic pain increase
annually even when they use lower reported figures to form their
estimates (p. 10).

The human dimensions of such statistics are the concern of pastors. The diversion of people from creative involvement in work,
meaningful pursuit of a life calling, and an unambivalent devotion
to that life calling are issues that underlie the astonishing dollar
estimates that Bonica gives. Obviously, ministry to people in pain
is not your central emphasis as a working pastor. However, it is
woven into the fabric of many of the central emphases of your work.
When chronic pain interferes with daily bread-winning, the involvement of that person in the life of the church suffers as well. The
hidden agenda in much interpersonal conflict in church and family
is the high irritability of persons in physical pain. Nonsensical behavior is more often motivated by pain than the casual observer
considers. In an era of pop psychologies, when even our bodily
movements are given covert interpretations, you may well ask
whether many of these movements are not the silent efforts of a
person to get into a position in which he or she will be in less pain.
In other words, you become a more discerning shepherd of your
flock when you have the skill, the information, and the perception
to assess the kinds and amounts of pain people suffer. A good
mother can separate the cries of her child and identify which is a
pain cry, which is a hunger cry, and which is a mischievous cry.
Similarly, as a pastor you can develop that kind of informed intui-
tion.

Wilbert Fordyce, an authority on the psychological aspects of
pain states in this country, gives a conceptualization of pain that
provides a helpful road map of the territory we plan to cover in the
following chapters. He says that chronic pain tends to ripple out
into larger and larger waves of complexity in a person's life. These
waves are depicted in Figure 1.

The initial wave is nociception, thermal or mechanical impingement on a nerve or a group of nerves. The second wave is pain itself,

the perception of impingement on the nerves. The third wave is suffering, negative emotional reactions brought about in higher nervous centers by the pain. The fourth wave is pain behavior, behavior that reflects the presence of nociception or nerve damage, such as speech, noise, facial expressions, seeking health care attention, and refusing to work. If you look at only one of these waves in action, and it is often separated from all the others, you do not grasp the whole process of pain the patient is experiencing.

FIGURE 1. Fordyce's four waves of pain.

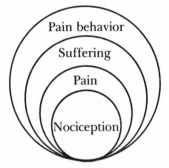

(Reprinted by permission of the publisher from "A Behavioral Perspective on Chronic Pain" by Wilbert Fordyce in Ng and Bonica, eds., *Pain, Discomfort, and Humanitarian Care*, p. 236. Copyright 1980 by Elsevier Science Publishing Co. Inc.)

On the basis of Fordyce's conceptualization, we can suggest three major pastoral strategies for relating effectively to a pain patient.

First, study carefully the language the person uses to describe his or her pain state. The McGill Pain Questionnaire in chapter 4 gives many examples of the kinds of language patients have been found to use. Learn the adjectives in the inventory and let them appear appropriately in a given interview. If you have a group or a longer-term counseling relationship, you may want to use the inventory as a paper-and-pencil exercise to give you a quicker assessment.

Second, observe the patient's bodily movements and compare—or contrast—them with the verbal descriptions. If, for example, a person complains of shoulder pain but reaches easily for a robe hanging on the wall, showing no evidence of pain, you have a contrast of behavior and language. If he or she guards that shoulder by using the other arm or asking you for help, you have consistency!

In the following three chapters, Charles Oates, a neurologist at the Rush-Presbyterian-St. Luke's Medical Center in Chicago, presents a detailed discussion of three important sets of data: the anatomy and neurochemistry of pain, the most common pain states and their causes, and the forms of treatment that physicians and other health care specialists provide. These presentations will enable you as a pastor to have a lay knowledge of what is going on medically with the parishioner, family member, or friend to whom you are ministering. Basic to this purpose is that you be an astute observer of these persons. Learn to listen with your eyes to what the person is doing as he or she talks about the pain. Such a skill will serve you in good stead in caring for people with any kind of difficulty.

Third, you will need detailed knowledge of the processes of pain and their medical care. The next three chapters take you into a vocabulary and discipline that may be somewhat novel. However, we are both convinced that if you will, as the *Book of Common Prayer* puts it, "read, mark, learn, and inwardly digest" the data being presented, you will be filled with wonder that, in spite of all the painful conditions that can afflict a human being, you yourself are as well as you are and that people with these conditions nevertheless can function at meaningful levels in spite of the pain they carry. Not all pain patients are on disability, and large numbers of them suffer without much notice being given by them to their pain. Yet if you develop the kind of understanding we are suggesting here, you will be appreciative in ways few people are. You will be sensitized to what social scientist Lillian Rubin calls the "worlds of pain" in which people live. You will be the *tebuna*, or person of understanding, who can draw them out of this private world into community with the people of God.

3

The Neurophysiology
of Pain

A neurologist or a neurophysiologist views pain differently from the way a lay person does. Besides the emotional perceptions that most people have, the neurologist is concerned with how pain is transmitted to the brain, the concept of **nociception**. Each physician is taught in medical school the classic pathways of sensory input, from the origin—say, at the fingertip that is traumatized by an ill-placed hammer blow—to the arrival in the consciousness of the unfortunate carpenter. However, much of what goes on between the blow of the hammer and the consequent burst of expletives has been explained in just the last thirty years.

The next three chapters describe these recent explanations of the origin, development, and treatment of pain, so that you, the pastor, may use the information to understand the patient's complaints and behavior, as well as the causes of pain and its treatment. This knowledge will foster an understanding relationship between physician, patient, pastor, and family members, for if each of these people is able to speak in the language of the others, all will benefit.

This chapter provides rather technical information about how pain is transmitted to and then processed by the brain. Unfortunately, this pill of information is somewhat bitter to swallow, and you may need to add some new words to your vocabulary. However, each word will be explained when it is used, and at the back of the book there is a short glossary of pain-relevant terms, identified in the text by boldface type the first time they appear.

Such information is vital to your understanding of how and why a patient has pain as a definable syndrome, even when there seems to be no good cause for a pain problem. Also, you will need a basic knowledge of the pathophysiology, or mechanism, of pain in order to understand the medical, behavioral, and psychological interventions prescribed to treat pain, which are described in chapter 5.

The Wiring Diagram of Pain

Let's start with the most basic building blocks and proceed from there. The *central nervous system* is composed of the brain, the spinal cord, and the brain stem, which connects them. The *peripheral nervous system* (PNS) is composed of those nerves that are outside the spinal cord and that conduct information to the spinal cord or away from it.

The fundamental building block of the body is the *cell.* Cells carry out specialized functions that sustain the organism to which they belong. Most organ systems have cells particular to that system. The CNS and PNS are no exceptions.

The specialized cell that makes up the nervous system is the **neuron.** The neuron collects information at one end and then electrically transmits that information to the other end, to discharge chemicals that can modify other areas of the organism, be it locally or at a distance (see Figure 2).

The receiving end of the neuron is called a **dendrite.** This is a spindly arm, attached to the neuron, with specialized endings that are able to convert information outside the neuron to a meaningful electrical message.

The heart of the neuron is the **cell body,** or **soma,** which contains the cell nucleus and the apparatus for chemical production. Without the cell body and nucleus, the whole neuron dies.

Extending from the cell body is a long projection called the **axon.** This is the telephone wire that carries encoded electrical information to its destination. The length may be microscopic or as long as the distance from the great toe to the top of the head. Surrounding this tubular structure is the **myelin sheath,** the equivalent of the plastic coating on an electrical wire. This structure is produced by another type of cell called a **Schwann cell.** Schwann cells form the insulation coating of the axon by wrapping themselves many times around the axon, which will look like a jelly roll if cut in cross-section.

The very tip of the axon is the business end; here, the axon communicates with other neurons. This structural region is called the **synapse.** In the synaptic ending are small spherical-shaped sacs containing chemicals used for communicating with the next nerve cell. These are called **neurotransmitters.** They transmit chemically encoded messages to near or distant sites. The usual function of the neurotransmitter is to excite a **receptor** on the next dendrite, so that the information is carried on down the neuron. The neurotransmitter works like a key in the receptor, which is like a lock. It takes the right key to fit the right lock. When the lock has the proper key in it, the neuron activates an electrical current that travels down its axon.

How does the process work? When the environment external to the neuron provides a stimulus that the specialized dendrites recognize, the receptor translates the information into an electrical signal

FIGURE 2. Anatomy of a neuron

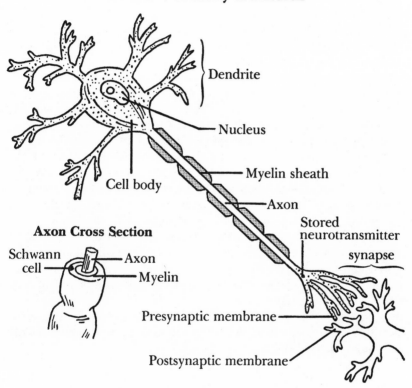

that is conducted down the axon to the synapse. At the synapse, the electrical impulse releases neurotransmitters at the **presynaptic** *membrane*. These diffuse to the **postsynaptic** *receptor* found on the next neuron's dendrite. With stimulation of this receptor, the signal travels through the next neuron in the same way.

The entire nervous system uses this basic structure to conduct its business. The process is the same, with elaborate variations and interactions, whether it initiates the blinking of an eye or the delivery of a homily. But *how* does this relate to the perception of pain?

It is important to understand the reason for the existence of pain in any organism. Pain is necessary to identify a noxious stimulus, its location, its temporal relationship, and its intensity, so that the organism may work either to avoid its occurrence or to escape its effects. Those things that cause or threaten tissue damage can lead to the death of the organism, and survival of the organism is a cardinal rule, in fact, pain is so essential to survival that, when normal pathways are destroyed, the body finds alternate pathways for nociception.

Perhaps the best way to understand the neuroanatomical pathway of nociception is to continue the simple illustration used at the start of this chapter of an acute painful sensation that most people have experienced. A man is hanging a picture by using a hammer and nail. Through inexperience or bad luck, the hammer finds the tip of his finger, instead of the nail head, and strikes the thumbnail. A fraction of a second elapses. Then the man realizes that something has happened: pain. A whole set of complex behaviors occur. Let's say he drops picture, nail, and hammer. He grabs his thumb with his other hand to hold and rub it. He speaks some words relating to the parentage of the hammer. In anger, he puts his foot through the painting, an emotional consequence of the pain. About this time the sharp, sudden pain changes to a pronounced dull or searing pain. The man paces the room, holding both hands together and shaking them. The pain resolves enough for him to realize that his painting has been destroyed. Then he realizes something else: financial loss associated with pain. But perhaps insurance will pay for it (reward for having pain).

With this scenario in mind, let us follow the process of nociception from thumb to brain, including the perceptual components of pain and related issues.

The Anatomical Pathway of Nociception

We have seen that the dendrite receives information from either the nearby or the distant environment. The dendrites beneath the skin are responsible for telling the first neuron in the pathway that something in the environment has changed. Specialized endings deduce what form of sensation has changed; that is, whether the change is thermal, mechanical (pressure), or chemical. Respectively, these are called *thermoreceptors, mechanoreceptors,* and *chemoreceptors.* Some endings sense only temperature, or pressure, or chemicals, but others are *polymodal receptors.* This last group will respond to strong temperature change, mechanical distortion, *or* chemical changes (like acids).

Each type of receptor is associated with a certain axon diameter. The diameter of the axon is determined by how many times it has been wrapped by the Schwann cell to form the myelin sheath. Some axons in the PNS are not wrapped by any myelin. The thicker the myelin, the faster the nerve can conduct its information to the synapse at the end of the axon. This speed is measured in meters per second. The faster a nerve conducts information, the earlier the information arrives at its destination. The axon and its sheath form the nerve fiber.

Nerve fibers are classified by how much myelin surrounds the axon, the *myelinization.* The classification is further based on the diameter of the axon. The basis of the classification system gives some sense to the otherwise unusual names of the fiber types. I will mention only the classes relevant to our discussion.

Fast and Slow Pain

The fiber that is associated with the greatest amount of myelinization is known as **A-delta fiber**. This fiber has a conduction speed of 6 to 20 meters per second and is usually connected to receptors that are mechanoreceptors, thermoreceptors, or polymodal receptors. This receptor-and-nerve combination is most important in transmitting information at a fast rate, which localizes the point of pain information. When these receptors are stimulated on their own, the pain is described as having a pricking quality that is attached to the specific body site of origin. In our example, the hapless hammerer knows without looking that he has struck his thumb. The sharp pain initially experienced is acute and known as **epicritic pain.**

The fibers or axons that do not have a myelin sheath have a slower conduction rate because myelin helps to speed the electrical conduction of information by insulating the axon. This size axon is called a **C fiber**. C fibers are associated with thermoreceptors and polymodal receptors (if the latter are stimulated with strong mechanical, chemical, or thermal stimuli). They conduct information at 1 meter per second. They help mediate slow pain known as **protopathic pain.**

Back to our example: the pain originating from C-fiber input accounts for the slower-arriving pain that is described as being dull or burning in nature and also persists after the sharp, fast pain has started to wane. Interestingly, this later pain is poor in its ability to show where it is coming from, compared to the pinpoint localization of input from the A-delta fiber.

The difference in conduction speed in certain pain-conducting nerves is felt to be the basis of two types of pain, **fast** or epicritic **pain** and **slow** or protopathic **pain**. When the picture hanger strikes his thumb with the hammer, the earliest, or fast, pain arrives at the consciousness immediately and is felt as the sharp, localized pain we call acute. Slow pain, which supplants the fast pain, is later in arriving in the awareness, for it is actually slower in getting to the spinal cord from the offended body area.

Locating and Tracing Pain's Origin

We have seen that the noxious stimulus of smashing one's thumb announces its presence to different receptors in the skin of the thumb. From there the information is carried along both A-delta and C fibers at different rates of conduction. The pain information is relayed on certain nerves that have their dendrites located in the thumb. (These main nerves have specific names. The one involved here is the *median nerve.* If the man had dropped the hammer on his toe, the sciatic nerve would have been the main pathway to the spinal cord.)

The information moves toward the spinal cord through the vertebral column, which forms the spinal cord's protective covering. There it passes by the neuron's cell body, which is located just inside the vertebral column (Figure 3).

Just outside the vertebral column, a grouping of nerve fibers and cell bodies forms a **ganglion**. The ganglions that are connected in a long chain running the length of the thorax and abdomen on either side of the vertebral column are called the **sympathetic ganglion** (see Figure 4). The sympathetic chain is involved in controlling blood-vessel diameter, sweating, and other functions.

These long strips of interconnected ganglions are arranged on the back internal surface of the body, which is described as the **dorsal** (or **posterior**) surface. The front part of the body (with the face and belly button) is called the **ventral** (or **anterior**) surface. This distinction in terminology helps us to picture the location of anatomical structures. Many structures have one of these words as part of its name.

The information continues toward the spinal column by using the incoming route beyond the dorsal cell body, in the *dorsal* (or posterior) *root.* The dorsal root carries primary sensory information into the spinal cord from the area of the body it serves. The nerve

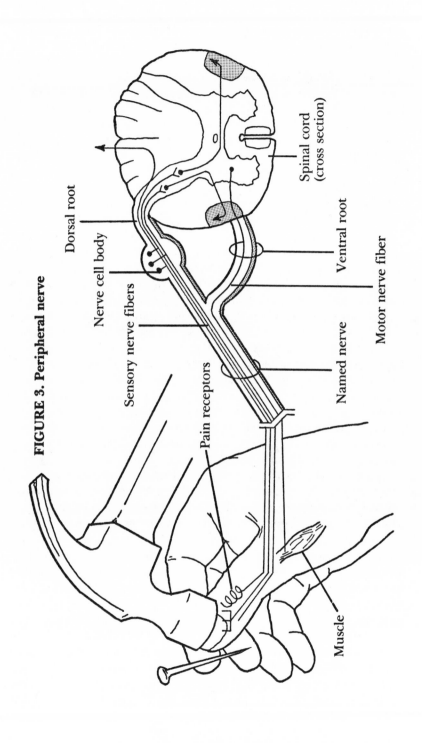

FIGURE 3. Peripheral nerve

Dorsal root

Nerve cell body

Sensory nerve fibers

Pain receptors

Muscle

Named nerve

Motor nerve fiber

Ventral root

Spinal cord
(cross section)

courses through the opening of the bony vertebral column, is changed in name to dorsal root, and then becomes incorporated in the spinal cord.

Take a moment now to inspect Figure 4. The spinal cord is represented by a cross-sectional view. This is what the cord looks like if you cut it perpendicular to its longest dimension. The overall pattern of an H is made up by the difference in the **gray matter** (made up of the nerve cell bodies) and the **white matter** (made up mostly of myelin-covered axons). The gray matter makes up an H pattern, with each leg of the H being called a horn, either ventral or dorsal, depending on its relationship to the rest of the body. The **ventral horn** contains the cell bodies of nerves that influence muscles by sending electrical information out the ventral root to the muscles. The **dorsal horn** contains nerve cell bodies of the neurons that receive sensory information from nerves originating in specific body areas, like the thumb of our hammer-wielding friend.

The white matter of the spinal cord is organized into *tracts*, which are like expressways running next to the ventral and dorsal horns. They carry information to and from the spinal cord levels, or segments, and to and from the brain. Tracts are named for their position, origin, and destination in the nervous system. Thus, the anterolateral tract is in the anterior and lateral region of the cord, the tract situated on the outermost edge of the cord's front surface. This tract conducts pain information from the spinal cord to the **thalamus**, a brain structure related to the appreciation of painful stimuli; anatomists named it the **anterolateral spinothalamic tract.** (A formidable word like this is easily deciphered by breaking it into its component parts.)

To recap, the nociceptive stimulus travels into the spinal cord by the dorsal sensory root. The dorsal horn of the gray matter in the spinal cord receives the information, then sends it to the spinothalamic tract to be conducted to the thalamus.

Of course, things aren't always as simple as they seem. So it is with the spinal cord transmission of pain. As the electrical stimulus is brought into the dorsal horn, it reaches the first synapse in the pathway. The information is conducted by neurotransmitters to the next neuron in the chain, which in turn sends the information to the opposite, or **contralateral**, spinothalamic tract. That tract is made of the axons of thousands of neurons involved in conducting information about pain from that point or below in the body up to the **ipsilateral** thalamus. Only a few of the neurons receiving pain information send their information up to the thalamus on the same side of the body as the source of the pain. These are pain fibers that

FIGURE 4. Cross section of spinal cord

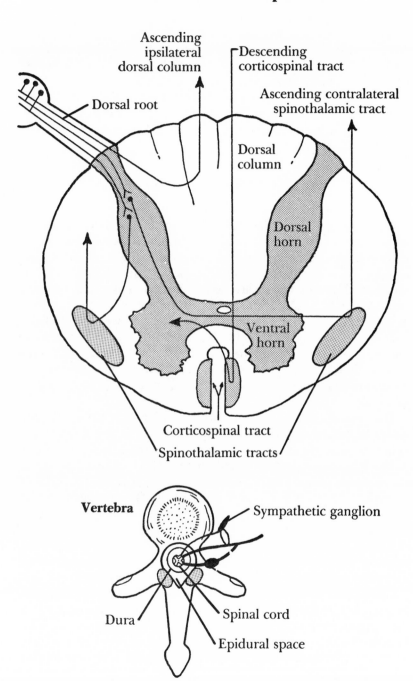

ascend on the same side or ipsilateral fiber tract, which is also called the anterior spinothalamic tract.

This information is basic to understanding how surgery has been used to treat pain by interrupting the flow of information from the source to the brain. Pain signals can be halted in their ascent by cutting the contralateral anterior spinothalamic tract at the level relevant to the origin of the pain. Unfortunately, as you now know, some pain fibers ascend ipsilaterally. These few fibers explain how the same pain can return in six months to two years after successful surgery for pain relief.

The Spinal-Cord Processing of Pain

The spinal cord works somewhat like a computer at each level. The second neuron in the pain pathway stands ready to fire off information to the higher levels of the brain, but before this occurs there is some processing of the information. In the region where the first neuron in the pain pathway reaches electrochemically to touch the second neuron, there are other neurons. The other neurons may have their origin in the same skin region (the thumb, in our example). Or they may originate at higher or lower levels of the body in the same general region (such as the shoulder or armpit in our example). Finally, neurons descend from the brain and brain stem to influence directly what information is sent "upstream." There are more neurochemicals active at this level, and they also influence the processing.

The central nervous system works at all levels by using the processes of **excitation** and **inhibition**. This means that a neuron is either stimulated to the point of discharge or negatively influenced so that it becomes less likely to discharge. This is done by changing the electrochemical environment around the neuron. The neuron essentially adds up the total number of excitatory influences and subtracts the inhibitory influences to determine its probability of discharge. If the sum total is toward excitation, the neuron will discharge and send an electrical impulse to the synapse. But if the negative or inhibitory influences are greater than the positive or excitatory influences, the neuron will remain quiescent.

Finally, this modulation of neuronal activity occurs in the pain pathway before the synapse. The modulating influence is exerted on the synaptic ending of the first neuron in the pain pathway. The information is processed before the second neuron's dendrite gets wind of any change in the environment. Figure 5 represents this concept by using positive and negative signs, as is the custom in neurology.

Melzack and Wall investigated spinal-level pain processing. They noted that if a painful region was rubbed, touched, or stimulated in a nonpainful manner, the manifest pain was much less. The investigators found that, during this subsequent stimulation, A-delta

FIGURE 5. The gate theory of pain control

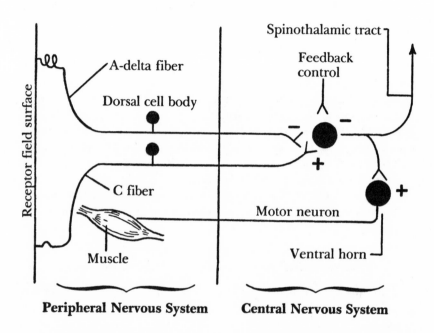

fibers were inhibiting C fibers from exciting the second neurons in the pain pathway. This means that information coming from the region where the pain originates has the ability to race ahead of the impulse from the slower C fibers and "gate out" the pain by keeping the next neuron quiescent. This is known as the **gate theory of pain control.**

An important active, naturally occurring protein was isolated in the dorsal horn area for pain processing. The material is called **substance P**. When this protein substance was experimentally placed in the posterior horn region of the spinal cord, the second neuron started firing. In fact, this chemical was produced by the

A-delta and C fibers when they were stimulated. Morphine, a potent narcotic medication, blocks the action of substance P. Capasaicin, a pain-causing material found in red chili peppers, was found to increase the secretion of substance P. This shows that pain has its own specific neurotransmitters, which help pass on information and influence the spinal level of pain processing.

Lastly, the spinal level of processing is the cause of a self-propagating form of chronic pain. As mentioned earlier, the ventral horn of the spinal cord contains the neurons responsible for exciting the muscles to contract. They receive their commands mostly from the **corticospinal tract** (see Figure 4), which conducts motor information signals from the cortex of the brain to the spinal-cord levels. But the ventral horn neurons also receive impulses from the second nerve in the pain pathway. The immediate loop of sensation → spinal cord → motor command allows us to pull our finger away from the hot stove without thinking about it. However, if painful stimuli continue to send information to the second neuron in the pathway, which in turn causes the muscles of the region to spasm, the spasm of the muscle will stimulate the pain receptors in the muscle. Hence, a vicious cycle is born that can lead to chronic pain: painful stimulus → neural activation of the first pain neuron → activation of the motor neuron → persistent contraction of the muscle to the point of spasm → pain → more stimulation of the pain pathway.

Conduction of Pain from Spinal Cord to the Brain

Our trip from thumb to brain has brought us to the ascent of the pain impulse to the brain stem, after being modified at the spinal level by presynaptic excitation or inhibition.

The anterolateral spinothalamic tract runs the whole length of the spinal cord. Pain signal information enters at each level along its course. The left anterolateral spinothalamic tract receives the majority of its fibers from the right side of the body but also carries a few fibers from the left side. The tract of myelinated fibers eventually courses through the brain stem, gives off branches to that area, and then arrives at the thalamus. The thalamus is another gray matter structure. It is located in the deep middle part of the brain next to the spinal fluid channels known as **ventricles**. Take the time now to study Figure 6.

The thalamus is a complex structure whose total function is beyond the scope of this book. It is considered part of the **limbic system**, the structures and tracts associated with sensation, mem-

FIGURE 6. Pathway of nociception

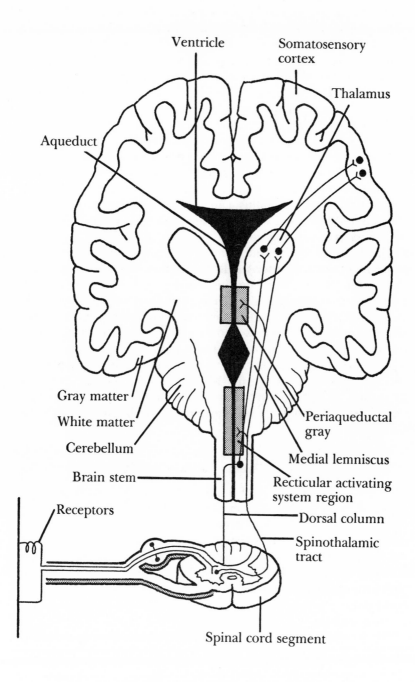

ory, and emotion. We are primarily interested in its emotion and sensation functions. In general, the thalamus receives a small percentage of all sensory information that arises from the spinal cord. (The greater percentage of information is diverted to the brain stem.)

After the information is partly modulated by the thalamus, it is relayed to the **cerebral cortex**, or surface region of the brain. Unfortunately, the thalamus is frequently subject to strokes or spontaneous bleeding. A specific stroke in the region of the thalamus associated with pain information processing will produce a severe chronic pain disorder called *thalamic pain syndrome*. This pain syndrome causes a person to perceive a trivial light touch as searing pain. Another concept emerges here: The body can fool itself into misinterpreting sensory information as being painful despite the benign nature of the stimulus. Later, we will see how this perception of stimuli also works in the opposite manner, so that pain is not perceived as something noxious.

The thalamus receives information from another tract that has yet to be mentioned. Those A-delta fibers that brought information from mechanoreceptors into the spinal cord have a tract of their own. The tract arises in the spinal cord on the same side as the sensory information entrance point and does not cross to the opposite side immediately. It is known as the **dorsal column**, for it remains on the dorsal (posterior) side of the spinal cord up to the level of the brain stem. At the brain-stem level it changes position and is then called the **medial lemniscus**. The medial lemniscus waits until the last minute to cross to the opposite side of the brain stem before it also gives off branches to the brain stem and the thalamus.

The Neospinal Pathway of Pain

At this part of our tour of the pain pathway, we are at the level of the thalamus as it sends its modulated pain information to the cortex of the brain, having received information from the anterior spinothalamic tract and the medial lemniscus. This part of the pathway is referred to as the **neospinal pathway**, for it has evolved only in higher-order vertebrates, specifically primates. The **paleospinal pathway**, or ancient pathway, involves the brain-stem route of pain processing. This latter pathway is present in both primate and nonprimate animals.

The neospinal pathway projects to the somatosensory cortex of the brain. A miniature representation of the whole body is present over the vertical length of this area. The representation is the greatest for the face, mouth, and hands and more limited for other body parts. Likewise, this representation is of the contralateral body surface, so that the *right* brain receives information about the *left* side of the body and vice versa.

The somatosensory cortex is responsible for the precise localization of sensory information. That is why you are aware without having to look that it is the middle of your thumbnail that has been smashed. This pinpoint pain is known as epicritic pain. A stroke involving only this cortex will leave the victim able to feel pain but unable to localize its specific area of origin. When pinched on the hand opposite the injured brain, the patient becomes aware that something has occurred, but slightly slower than a normal person would, and may grope for the cause of pain on the normal side of the body. After not finding the source, the patient will search the chest, the shoulder, and then the arm on the correct body side until the hand and the noxious stimulus are found accidentally.

One last note on the cortical representation of pain. Pain from one side of the body reaches predominantly the opposite side of the brain, but it also reaches the same side. This is why cutting out small areas of the somatosensory cortex is not an appropriate therapy for chronic pain syndromes. If that is done, the pain is still perceived with the same intensity, for it travels to lower levels of the same brain hemisphere, to the opposite hemisphere, and to the paleospinal pathway.

The Paleospinal or Ancient Pathway of Pain

We have now completed the pathway of neospinal nociception. Earlier, we said that the spinothalamic tract gave off branches to a different pathway at the level of the brain stem. If the brain is viewed as a large mushroom, the brain stem is analogous to the mushroom's stem. Refer to Figure 6.

The brain stem contains neurons that are responsible for breathing, blood pressure, temperature, and level of arousal. A stroke in the area related to arousal will render a person permanently unconscious, whereas neurochemical alterations in the same area will cause the person to be hyperalerted and unable to sleep. This same area is intimately involved with the pain pathway. It is known as the *reticular activating system.* The reticular activating system receives and regulates the nociceptive input from the spinothalamic pain.

The brain stem also houses a fluid-filled channel that is continuous with the ventricles spoken of earlier. These channels contain *cerebrospinal fluid,* the material obtained when a person has a spinal tap or lumbar puncture. The continuity of the ventricular system that runs through the center of the brain stem is known as the **aqueduct,** like the water supply of the Romans, for it carries spinal fluid from the upper protion of the brain, where it is made, to the lower regions of the brain stem and spinal cord.

Neurons surround the aqueduct and are called the **periaqueductal gray** (see Figure 6). They produce a neurotransmitter called **serotonin,** or **5-hydroxytryptamine,** a chemical that is important in the communication of one nerve with another. Serotonin is important in the limbic pathways associated with emotion and sleep, pathways we will refer to as a whole for the sake of simplicity. Serotonin-deficient states are associated with depression. Some antidepressant medications restore serotonin to the central nervous system. When this is done, depression that is not a reaction to a trauma will abate.

Now that you have worked through this additional information, we may discuss the paleospinal pathway of pain in a more effective way. We left the ascent of the pain information at the level of the spinothalamic tract in the brain stem. Most of the spinothalamic tract separates from the smaller branch (which goes to the thalamus) and goes to the brain stem, ultimately ending in the regions of the periaqueductal gray and the reticular activating system. From that point there is continuity of the signal into the limbic system.

Through the paleospinal pathway of pain we derive several characteristics of pain perception. If a painful stimulus occurs when a person is asleep, the spinal-level processing causes him or her to withdraw from the cause reflexively. The second is an alerting response; that is, the person awakens. This is mediated by the reticular activating system.

Each of us has an emotional reaction to pain. A baby cries. A football player gets mad and hits something. Even an Indian guru appreciates the stimulus as painful, though he may not display emotion. The paleospinal pathway is responsible, in part, for these emotional consequences, and they occur even if the neospinal pathway is cut.

The paleospinal system distributes pain derived from the C fibers on one side of the body in such a fashion that both sides of the brain receive the information; in other words, bilateral representation. (You will recall that neospinal representation is predominantly unilateral.) The paleospinal system accounts for the stroke patient's perceiving pain as being irritating but possibly on the opposite side from its origin.

So it may be said that when the paleospinal system is experimentally isolated, it gives rise to diffuse, poorly localized bilateral sensation of C-fiber-mediated pain, pain that has an emotional component of anxiety and restlessness. This describes protopathic pain.

Descending Influence of Pain Upon the Spinal Cord

The human body is resplendent with systems of feedback. The body must know if the adjustments made in a system are working too little, enough, too much, or not at all. If too little, the system should be alerted to continue in a given process. If too many effects are observed by the feedback, then the system must stop itself from continuing the action. This latter concept is known as **feedback inhibition**, for the feedback itself stops the process.

Examples of feedback inhibition include the actions of the **pituitary** gland in relation to hormonal production, the movement of ingested food through the bowel as related to the churning motions of the stomach, and the control of pain information at the level of the spinal cord.

The higher levels of the CNS have the ability to control lower levels of the system by the process of feedback inhibition. In this way the body controls pain by not allowing itself to receive the information into either paleospinal or neospinal pathways. The mechanism is as follows:

The spinothalamic tract sends information concerning a noxious stimulus into the reticular activating system. In response, the cells of this system produce serotonin, which eventually helps inhibit the first pain pathway neuron as it enters the dorsal horn. This affects a presynaptic inhibition of that neuron, for it is less likely to alert the next neuron in the pain pathway.

The motor cortex and the somatosensory cortex have direct feedback neurons that descend from those two different areas to the dorsal horn at all levels of the spinal cord. These fibers have the ability to excite or inhibit the neurons in the dorsal horn.

Finally, the motor neurons (those nerves responsible for activating muscles) are able to excite or inhibit dorsal horn pain fibers by collateral branches at each spinal level. The motor neurons descend from the motor cortex to specific spinal levels to affect specific muscle groups. You will recall that pain fibers have collateral branches that influence the motor fibers. This constitutes a feedback loop, for each component has the opportunity to tell the other components what has occurred and to regulate the process of those related neurons.

There is another mechanism the higher brain uses to control pain information at the central and spinal levels. But before that story may be told, we must discuss some data that are on the frontier of pain therapy research.

The Endogenous Pain Control System

In the last decade, researchers have been exploring a curiosity that had been known for some time. Morphine, the gold standard of potent narcotics, has specific receptors in many parts of the CNS. When given to a patient in pain, morphine finds these receptors and fits into them much like a key in its lock.

The curiosity was this: Why should there be a preexisting receptor for a man-made chemical? A hunt was undertaken for this naturally occurring key, and one was found. In fact, more than one.

The group of compounds that fit these receptors was named **endorphins**, or "opiates from within." Endorphins are proteins that look very much like beta lipotropin, an already known hormone, and are actually the last few **amino acids** of the beta lipotropin chain. (The experimenters obtained endorphins for laboratory use from the pituitary of the camel, an animal renowned for its indifference to pain.)

An injection of endorphins has the same effect as an injection of morphine, and both produce tolerance and withdrawal if given long enough. (*Tolerance* means that increasing doses are needed to achieve the same effect if the drug is administered over a long period of time, because the body develops more efficient methods of breaking down the medication.) Endorphin receptors are located in the periaqueductal gray region, those lower levels of the brain stem associated with blood pressure and temperature regulation, in the neurons of the dorsal horn, and in the adrenal gland. They are produced in the periaqueductal gray region, in the **hypothalamus** (the fight-or-flight gland in the brain), and in the anterior pituitary (this master gland is divided into front and back sections that have distinctively different functions and products).

Much of the research into these receptors and compounds is accomplished by using a clinically available medication called **naloxone**. This drug enters the nervous system and replaces any morphine, morphinelike drug, endorphin, or enkephalin at its receptor site. It is used clinically to reverse the effects of morphine overdose. A person comatose from morphine will awaken and start breathing independently in seconds after injection with naloxone.

Experimentally, naloxone is used to determine the presence or absence of endorphin-mediated pain modulation. If given after a medication or other pain-relieving measure, the return of the pain to pretreatment levels is indicative of endorphin-mediated analgesia.

Through these different experimental designs, much has been learned. Endorphins are increased during electrical stimulation, adequate treatment of depression, adequate treatment of chronic pain through pharmacologic or nonpharmacologic means, activation of descending control of the dorsal horn pain fibers, use of placebo "medications" or manipulations, and physical exercise training.

A point worth repeating is that the endorphin system is the final pathway for the descending control of pain and is similar to serotonin and direct projections from the motor and sensory cortices.

Endorphins are decreased in chronic pain states and morphine addiction. They are also ineffective without the presence of serotonin.

It is easy to see why a chronic pain patient may be endogenously depressed, because the depletion of endorphins correlates with the depression, as does the depletion of serotonin. Conversely stated, depressed patients may experience more pain-related disorders because the depletion of serotonin in depression also renders the depleted endorphins less effective.

This discussion of the neurochemistry of pain completes the preliminary tour of the pain pathway. You have been taken through the basic neuroanatomy and neurophysiology of pain. Your new level of understanding allows us to continue discussing the most recent literature on pain and its therapy.

Pain as a Learned Behavior

Pain is a physiological phenomenon. Even the lowest forms of life show a response to nociception. Higher levels have the ability to learn. The Russian physiologist Pavlov paired the sound of a bell with the presentation of food to his dogs. This connection eventually was learned, so that when the bell rang without the presentation of food, the dog salivated anyway. This form of learning is now called classical **respondent conditioning,** for the response to a discriminative stimulus, the bell, is primarily a reflex response.

The acute pain that our hapless hammerer experienced has resulted in a set of responses that are based on reflexes associated with pain. First, he drops the hammer and grabs his injured thumb. The withdrawal of the injured hand is reflexive, albeit mediated by a mechanism of nociception processing at the level of the spinal cord. Associated with the initial injury are the reflexive responses of increased heart rate, dry mouth, increased sweating, and pupillary dilation. If the hammer even comes close to hitting his finger again, each of these respondent behaviors will follow suit, because our friend has learned from his last experience. Acute pain has many other respondent behaviors that are learned and are associated with its occurrence.

Chronic pain, because of its duration, has fewer respondent behaviors associated with the baseline pain level; operantly conditioned behaviors are more characteristic of such long-lasting pain. These behaviors are usually mediated by skeletal muscles, because a person must move to receive the reinforcement. Reinforcers given after a behavior has occurred condition the subject to repeat that behavior so as to receive the reinforcement again.

For example, take a young boy who dearly loves bakery cookies. The first time his mother brought them home he was unaware of what was in the white bakery box. After seeing the box open with his favorite cookies inside, he could identify this "discriminative stimulus." The next time his mother came home with a similar box, he exhibited an operantly conditioned behavior: he picked up his toys without being told, to curry favor with his mother and receive a cookie. The cookie is the reward or reinforcer of the conditioned behavior of clearing away his toys, behavior exhibited only upon presentation of the discriminative stimulus, the white box.

Chronic pain similarly induces a myriad of complex behaviors and social interactions that evolve by **operant conditioning** superimposed upon the personality of the patient and behaviors the patient has previously learned. Pain has reflexive behaviors associated with it, but most of what happens as a consequence of pain is learned behavior.

Pain behavior refers to all forms of behavior generated by the individual that are commonly understood to reflect the presence of nociception. These include facial expression, posture, seeking medical attention, taking medications, and refusing to work or to engage in social activities.

Chronic pain by definition has lasted longer than two weeks. The average patient who is troubled with persistent pain has had the pain for months to years. The longer the pain persists, the more entrenched the pain-related behaviors become. In fact, in most cases, if the pain were suddenly gone, the behaviors would persist, for the reinforcements are many and mighty. This persistence of pain in the absence of nociception is known as *operant pain*.

The most common form of chronic pain is low back pain. Besides being a frequent injury that is not easily rectified by many therapies, there are other reasons it is a significant problem. Persons with chronic pain may be offered a life-style that does not require that they work to be paid, one in which they are not required to engage in activities they deem unsuitable. They are given medications that ensure a warm fog of euphoria and sedation, and they are treated in an ingratiating manner. Presented in that manner, who would not go through a few barium enemas to assure those reinforcers? Thus it is not so outlandish to have the reinforcers continue pain-related behaviors even though nociceptive input has ceased.

This relatively simple picture of operant conditioning will help you, the pastor, in helping your parishioner. By identifying environmental reinforcers, you can do much to break the cycle of maladaptive behavior. As an observant pastor, you will be able to discern the rewards that are achieved by the persistence of pain behaviors.

Emotions Associated with Nociception: Conditioned Behavior or Anatomically Preprogrammed Behavior?

As humans, we associate emotions with information learned and acts undertaken. So it is with pain. Anxiety is the hallmark of anticipated pain. Going to the dentist is feared by many because that ritual is known for inducing pain. A child who has not experienced the pain associated with being injected with novocaine for a dental procedure does not have the fear or the anxiety associated with the initial pain upon injection. From this we can say that anxiety is a learned behavior or emotion associated with pain.

Anxiety affects many of the behaviors associated with pain. Talking about one's nociception or malady is a pain behavior. Experiments show that the frequency with which verbal pain is reported is correlated with increased anxiety. Conversely, as anxiety decreases, so do the pain reports. Increasing levels of anxiety are associated with decreased effectiveness of pain therapy. When anxiety is reduced, the efficacy of pain therapy increases. This is one of the reasons that **anxiolytic medications** such as diazepam (Valium) or chlordiazepoxide (Librium) are frequently used as adjunctive therapy, because the addition of these medications breaks the cycle of pain → anxiety → increased pain → increased anxiety.

Anxiety has its origin in the limbic system. Anxiolytic medications like Valium exert their effects in this system. Some persons are "born worriers." Psychiatrists and neurobehaviorists question whether there is some anatomical or neurochemical predisposition to anxiety. We know that strokes in very specific areas of the brain will leave persons with little care about their surroundings. Persons with right hemisphere strokes, especially frontal lobe strokes, are known for apathy toward their deficit or toward attempts at rehabilitation. This is a vast region of research that is far from being unraveled to anyone's satisfaction. Shall we conclude that the emotion of anxiety both occurs naturally and is learned?

Insensitivity to Pain

What of the other perceptions concerning pain? We know that there are wide variations in how people handle pain, from cry babies to stoics. Why are there such differences?

Some persons actually are totally indifferent to pain. This does not mean that they don't feel the same stimulus that we would label as painful. They just do not perceive the stimulus as noxious. They are able to feel all the subtleties in sensation. Upon autopsy of these rare individuals, nothing abnormal is found. These patients have this "disorder" of pain perception from birth, so they are examples of **congenital indifference to pain.**

Though being indifferent (not insensitive) to pain sounds great at first, it has its problems. One of my patients had this disorder of pain perception. She might rest her hand on a red-hot burner while stirring a pot on the other side of the stove. She was unconcerned about the tissue damage to her burnt hand. In another instance, when she broke her nondominant arm in two places, she was not interested in seeking medical attention until she missed the function of the arm! Many patients with congenital indifference to pain eventually die from complications associated with persistent trauma to the limbs.

Investigators ask whether the experiences reported by these patients with **algoanosia** (the inability to understand pain) are even the same experience as pain. Curiously, the only uncomfortable sensation that these patients report is of mild frontal headaches. Is it *pain* they are experiencing and reporting?

Persons unlucky enough to have a stroke in the dominant hemisphere (the one responsible for language, usually the left hemisphere), in the region that contains fibers projecting from the sensory cortex to the limbic system acquire an insensitivity to pain. Stimulation of pain receptors is projected into the sensory cortex, but the information doesn't travel from the sensory cortex to the structures associated with emotion. These patients show none of the facial or gross motor behaviors associated with pain, but their heart rate, sweating, and pupillary reactions to pain are intact. This disorder has been called **pain asymbolia.**

Some persons with severe mental deficiency are known to have a relative indifference to pain. Whether this is mediated by their otherwise poor reporting of the internal environment or is a function of an altered pain threshold has not been completely explained. Also, hysterical patients with conversion reactions have long been known for their ability to tolerate extreme pain in their "affected" body regions.

The perception of pain may exist beyond the removal of a body part. Persons with a limb amputated will complain of a perception that the limb is still present. They are able to feel the position, weight, movements, and shape of the limb despite acknowledging its absence. These are known as *phantom limb sensations.* Such persons are subject to *phantom limb pain syndrome,* a horrible chronic pain syndrome associated with the amputated limb. There is very little effective therapy for this condition.

Finally, another well-known alteration of pain perception is seen in trauma or in patients wounded in battle. Severe significant wounds may go unnoticed for long periods during the heat of combat or until the threatening environment quietens. This effect is not mediated by the endorphin system, for it is not blocked by naloxone in experimental trials. It is thought to be due to a hormonally mediated mechanism.

Pain Thresholds

Why are some persons stoical about pain, whereas others crumble in the face of trivial discomfort? Part of this question is answered by the theory of the **pain threshold.**

Pain threshold is the level of stimulus intensity at which a person reports pain. The measurement depends on the person's report of his or her internal environment. We have no other way of measuring pain.

A high threshold for pain means that a person can tolerate a more severe stimulus before labeling that stimulus as painful. A low pain threshold implies reporting of pain at a lower stimulus intensity.

Patients over sixty complained less often of pain than did younger patients used as control subjects. Both increasing age and a reluctance of the elderly to label a stimulus as painful correlate with a higher pain threshold.

The lay opinion that women have a higher threshold for pain is not experimentally borne out. Tolerance to pain was greater in men. Women tended to complain more readily and received analgesics earlier, but they sustained longer relief from their medications.

Pregnancy affords the mother an increased pain threshold beginning four days before the child's birth. The threshold doubles at 24 to 48 hours before delivery and returns to baseline by 14 days afterward. This effect was eliminated by naloxone.

Pain thresholds are lowered in the late afternoon, independent of the patient's mood. Conversely stated, the analgesic effect of medications was most pronounced during the morning and the hours just after midnight.

During sleep there is a period when the muscles are relaxed but the eyes move rapidly. That period is called REM sleep, which stands for "rapid eye movement" and is necessary to maintain a normal mental state. People deprived of REM sleep have a reduced pain threshold that is independent of their increased irritability and mental disturbance.

As mentioned, anxiety lowers the pain threshold. Also, any pain perceived by an anxious person is remembered as being more intense. This is another area where the actions of a knowledgeable pastor can actually reduce pain in a quantifiable manner.

Finally, exercise programs that increase physical tolerance will increase the tolerance of pain. Physical activity is something that reduces the pain perceived and can be another of your positive pastoral interventions.

A Summary of the Process of Pain

Bear with me for one last review. We will return to the hapless hammer user. Upon the impact of the hammer on his thumb, our friend initiated a series of neural events that ran in the following sequence. (It may help you to follow this summary if you refer back to figures 2 to 6.)

The pressure and temperature of the hammer head stimulates specialized skin mechanoreceptors, thermoreceptors and polymodal receptors. These receptors send their electrical information to the spinal cord via C and A-delta fibers. Just inside the dorsal root inside the vertebral column, the pain signal passes the cell body of the neuron. The signal reaches the dorsal horn of the spinal cord by way of the dorsal sensory root. At the same spinal level, the information is modulated by presynaptic inhibition, caused by

A-delta fiber gating, descending motor nerves, and the endorphin system associated with serotonin.

Next, the modulated nociception is sent to the brain-stem level via both ipsilateral and contralateral anterolateral spinothalamic fiber tracts. The mechanoreceptors send much of their information via the dorsal columns to the medial lemniscus and then to the thalamus. Both systems give off collateral fibers to the brain-stem regions known as the reticular activating system and the periaqueductal gray. The rest of the signal is sent to the thalamus.

The thalamus modulates the pain, then sends the information to both the limbic system and the somatosensory cortex. The spino-thalamic tract and the somatosensory cortex are considered the neospinal pain pathway, which is responsible for the epicritic, or "fine pricking," sensation of pain that helps in pain localization.

The brain-stem pathway mentioned is considered the paleospinal pain pathway. It is responsible for burning, persistent pain, with its concomitant emotional components, known as protopathic pain. This region is one of several that produce serotonin, endorphin, and enkephalin, the body's own pain-killing substances.

The human body's own pain regulation system explains the presence of naturally occurring opiate receptors at all levels of the neural axis. The endorphin mechanism alters our perception of pain at both the brain-stem and spinal levels. Naloxone helps to differentiate endorphin-mediated analgesia, such as placebo effect, from other causes.

Through these pathways the carpenter realizes that an injurious stimulus has happened. Reflexive or respondent behaviors then result; increased heart rate, pupillary dilation, and sweating are some examples. Rapid hand withdrawal is reflexive, because the pain receptor fibers directly excite the motor neurons that control the arm muscles.

Pain behaviors are learned, also. When the picture-hanger jumps back in pain, he learns to grasp his hurt thumb and to rub the offended region. This relieves pain via stimulation of A-delta fibers, which presynaptically inhibit C-fiber firing. This is the gate theory of pain modulation.

Other learned behaviors that occur in this example include the expletives repeated upon impact, the anxiety over hitting the thumb again, the sorrow over the damaged artwork, and seeking either medical or emotional support from those nearby.

Congratulations! You have successfully swallowed the bitter pills of neuroanatomy and neurophysiology. Use the up-to-date information in this chapter for reference. It will allow you to converse knowledgeably about pain with the patient, the physician, and members of the family. Most important, the next chapters are predicated upon this fundamental knowledge.

4

The Clinical Assessment of Pain and Chronic Pain Syndromes

Pain is the source of much consternation to both physician and patient. The myth accepted by both is that pain must come from some definable cause or lesion and should be treatable by either medicine or surgery. If dealt with properly, there should be no pain.

The patient is a product of our society that teaches this myth. We are all products of our pill-popping culture, which promises instant and total pain relief and a cure for every symptom. If the cause cannot be found, all that is needed is a more competent doctor or another thorough investigation. The patient knows "there must be something wrong" if there is pain.

The physician not only accepts this myth but helps keep it in force. Investigations are repeated time and time again, often to no avail. When no "cause" is found, the physician writes off the patient as a crock or a malingerer or makes a psychiatric referral. In essence, the victims are blamed for believing what they have been taught, that all pain must have an organic cause.

The task of clinical assessment of pain disorders brings to mind one of the seven labors of Hercules: cleaning the Augean stables. Hercules eventually solved his problem by diverting a major river through the stables, but our technology in the assessment of pain is not up to diverting creeks, much less rivers.

This chapter is designed to acquaint you with the methods used to assess pain and with some of the organic or "real" causes of pain. It can be read now and can also be referred to when medical topics related to pain occur later. The list of pain-related disorders is not complete but should be adequate for reference use. An additional source of accessible information is contained in the *Merck Manual*, an often-updated compilation of diagnosis and therapy, which can be borrowed from a library or bought in a bookstore.

Why Are Pain Disorders So Hard to Evaluate?

The description of pain and its qualities is elusive. In an interview with an elderly farmer, I asked him what kind of pain he had in his neck. He replied slowly, "Well, it's a *hurtin'* pain!" His facial expression implied that he could not believe someone would ask such a silly question.

This anecdote points up two observations: All providers of care must rely on the patient's verbal report to assess the presence, severity, and quality of pain; and reports of pain depend upon the patient's ability to be introspective, objective, and articulate.

The verbal reports offered by pain patients are tempered by their ability to use the language. The language of a farmer is not the same as that of a physician or pastor. Communication with a patient must be in words that are commonly understood and make sense, and it must be based upon no education other than what we get by living in this world. Subtleties of language work only with those persons who possess a large vocabulary.

The temperament of the person determines how much prodding, questioning, and investigation will be tolerated. Pain shortens even saintly dispositions. A short temper leads to more misunderstanding and less accurate medical care. Conversely, stoicism may be misleading, because therapeutic and diagnostic criteria may be overlooked when the inquiring medical care provider only receives "Oh, I'm fine," from the patient who is being questioned.

An obstetrician-in-training in Maine commented once that the stoicism of Down-Easters not infrequently prevented her from assessing the extreme pain related to inflamed abdomens. She said that her patients referred to that sharp, cutting pain as "just uncomfortable."

At the opposite end of the spectrum are those patients who perceive *any* pain as excruciating. When given a rating scale of 1 to 10, with 10 being the worst pain possible, they usually tell you "Eleven." If you ask while the pain is occurring, the number may still be 11, but you will notice that they tell you with a smile and can carry on a pleasant conversation without any distraction.

Another pitfall in pain assessment is seen in disorders that manifest themselves by the complaint of organic-sounding pain but do not have pain from an identifiable cause. **Briquet's syndrome** is one primarily of women who experience severe bodily pain as the major manifestation of a psychic disorder. These persons will usually complain of abdominal pain. Their complaint is very real to them, so real that they have usually had many abdominal operations by age fifty—all normal in their findings.

Given these problems, how then do we find out who is in pain, why they hurt and how badly, and what the etiology of their pain syndrome is?

Observable Signs of Pain

The behavioral approach to pain described in chapter 3 follows a good principle. What patients say about their pain should be considered as a behavior. Yet we should attend to *all* the behaviors associated with pain; words are only one.

Physicians look for *signs* of pain, objective evidence revealed by examination, as opposed to subjective *symptoms,* which are what the patient perceives and describes. As a pastor you can do this too, with practice. This section, therefore, concentrates on signs, not symptoms.

The wise observer attends not only to what is said but to how it is said. Pain patients may have a sense of urgency in their voice or, conversely, a sparseness to the flow of words. The voice may have hints of slurring, as from the side effects of medication or from substance abuse. The mouth may be dry, as in fright, so that a clicking sound results. Grunting, either loud or barely audible, is a hint of ongoing pain.

Facial expressions are important clues. The pain patient during active pain shows a furrowed brow, increased sweating, and dilation of the pupils. The color of the face may range from ashen whiteness to the red of blood suffused from subvocal grunting.

Ongoing pain has its own choreography. Patients with low back pain have a hard time sitting still, because there is an imaginary hot poker sticking them in the back and running down the leg. They move in the chair often or rise from the chair at socially inappropriate times. Some patients will assume a reclining position at any opportunity.

Neurologists are taught how to make diagnoses based in part on the manner in which a person walks; we describe a protective gait that "favors" or acts as a splint for a painful area as **antalgic**. Other movements may be similarly antalgic. The patient with low back pain doesn't bend forward, lean to the side, or suddenly move the affected region, because that increases the pain. A painful dominant arm forces a right-hander to eat with the left hand.

Another movement in the dance of pain is to place a hand on the affected body part. Behaviorists have noted this as a signal in carefully cataloging pain-related actions. It correlates well with increased pain and with reduction of pain.

Pain is very distracting. It interrupts the flow of thought. Often a conversation is halted in the middle as the pain patient stares blankly. Patients will complain of memory trouble and impaired concentration on detail work. This is the case whether they are asked to perform a prolonged task or even a simple one.

Unfortunately, none of these signs is infallible. Other disease states can masquerade behind the same signs. Getting used to a pain-ridden state may distort the physiological and psychological signs of pain. Medications frequently alter the baseline observations so they lose their usefulness as objective parameters. For these reasons, other scales or methods have been devised to measure pain.

Quantifiable Measures of Pain

Despite the obvious problems in assessing the presence and extent of pain, there are some ways to measure what is happening in the patient's body.

Earlier, we discussed an easy method of clinical assessment using a scale of 1 to 10 in each interview with a chronic pain patient. The 10 is the worst pain imaginable. Let me emphasize the word *imaginable*, for the 10 should relate to a severe pain that the patient can understand from past experience—perhaps slamming one's finger in a door, which has happened to most of us at one time or another.

Each person is his or her own control, and each time the rating method is used, the measurement is related to previous ratings. This is important, for one person's 5 may be another person's 2. It is the relationship of one day to the next that is important, not the absolute number obtained.

The patient who has trouble with abstraction and the patient who is given to embellishing and amplifying symptoms will require more instruction in the use of this scale. The usual responses from such persons are "I don't know" and "Eleven," respectively. Teach them by giving a verbal menu of examples, such as a hangnail equals 1 and bumping one's head hard on a cabinet is a 5.

Visual Analogue Scale

An extrapolation of the 1 to 10 scale is the visual analogue scale (Figure 7).

FIGURE 7. Visual analogue scale

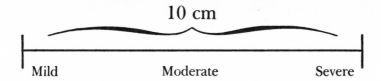

This is a ten-centimeter scale with pain-severity adjectives written on the bottom line from left to right. The left end is equivalent to 1 and the right end to 10. The patient is asked to make a hatch mark .on the line at the level of pain being experienced. A fresh line is presented during each interview and is then compared with those previously plotted. Some clinicians use a line without the words written across the bottom line, for the blank line allows less memory of previously plotted lines.

Minnesota Multiphasic Personality Inventory (MMPI)

This is a standard pencil-and-paper test used in psychometric investigation. A series of questions is presented to the patient. The patient is asked to agree or disagree with statements that range through activities, attitudes, and preferences.

This test is valuable in determining the patient's predilection for somatic disorders, somatization, depression, neuroses, and thought disorders. These characteristics are important in tailoring an effective treatment program and determining why a program may fail.

McGill Pain Questionnaire (MPQ)

This questionnaire was designed by a leading pain research team located at McGill University in Montreal. It is also a pencil-and-paper test. The patient is presented with a set of adjectives that describe the pain experience. Ronald Melzack, who helped design the questionnaire, describes the words as reflecting three main components: sensory, affective, and evaluative (see sample on page 60).

This questionnaire enables the user to standardize the language of pain and then measure the terms in order to come up with a dependent variable. As the experience of chronic pain changes, so does the score from the questionnaire.

The McGill Pain Questionnaire

What Does Your Pain Feel Like?

Some of the words below describe your *present* pain. Circle *only* those words that best describe it. Leave out any category that is not suitable. Use only a single word in each appropriate category—the one that applies best.

1. Flickering Quivering Pulsing Throbbing Beating Pounding	2. Jumping Flashing Shooting	3. Pricking Boring Drilling Stabbing Lancing	4. Sharp Cutting Lacerating
5. Pinching Pressing Gnawing Cramping Crushing	6. Tugging Pulling Wrenching	7. Hot Burning Scalding Searing	8. Tingling Itchy Smarting Stinging
9. Dull Sore Hurting Aching Heavy	10. Tender Taut Rasping Splitting	11. Tiring Exhausting	12. Sickening Suffocating
13. Fearful Frightful Terrifying	14. Punishing Grueling Cruel Vicious Killing	15. Wretched Blinding	16. Annoying Troublesome Miserable Intense Unbearable
17. Spreading Radiating Penetrating Piercing	18. Tight Numb Drawing Squeezing Tearing	19. Cool Cold Freezing	20. Nagging Nauseating Agonizing Dreadful Torturing

How Does Your Pain Change with Time?

1. Which word or words would you use to describe the *pattern* of your pain?

Continuous	Rhythmic	Brief
Steady	Periodic	Momentary
Constant	Intermittent	Transient

2. What kind of things *relieve* your pain?

3. What kind of things *increase* your pain?

How Strong Is Your Pain?

People agree that the following five words represent pain of increasing intensity. They are:

1. Mild   2. Discomforting   3. Distressing
4. Horrible   5. Excruciating

To answer each question below, write the number of the most appropriate word in the space beside the question.

1. Which word describes your pain right now?   _____

2. Which word describes it at its worst?   _____

3. Which word describes it when it is least?   _____

4. Which word describes the worst toothache you ever had?   _____

5. Which word describes the worst headache you ever had?   _____

6. Which word describes the worst stomachache you ever had?   _____

(Reprinted by permission of the author and the publisher, Elsevier Biomedical Press, from "The McGill Pain Questionnaire: Major Properties and Scoring Methods" by Ronald Melzack. *Pain*, vol. 1, p. 281, 1975.)

Behavioral Assessment of Pain

The behavioral approach to quantifying what a patient with chronic pain feels counts that patient's pain-related behaviors during a given time period. This requires skilled observers to watch the patient, either during the actual interview or afterward via videotape recordings.

Behaviors counted include touching the affected body part; an antalgic gait or gross movement of the body member that signals discomfort; grimacing, gritting the teeth, frowning, lip biting; and smiling. These four classes of behavior correlate best with therapy success or failure.

A Lay Person's Directory of Chronic Pain Syndromes

The following annotated list of chronic pain disorders is arranged by body area and organ system. The explanations of the symptoms and functional changes are summaries, not complete explanations. Use this list for reference. Once a summary explanation is under your belt, you will better understand the more comprehensive descriptions found elsewhere.

Low Back Pain

The *sine qua non* of back pain is the slipped disk or pinched nerve, otherwise known as a *herniated disk* or **radicular back pain**. Disks are cushions, found between the vertebrae, that are slightly thinner than the bone; viewed from above, they look like jelly doughnuts. When abnormal pressures or congenital malformations place stress on a disk, the "jelly" blows out on the side closest to where the spinal nerve leaves the vertebral column. This traps the nerve against the bone. The part "pinched" is the radicle; hence the name.

The person with radicular back pain complains of pain coming from the low back region and radiating down the leg to any of various levels. Frequently, the pain shoots to the foot like a hot poker. There may be a tingling sensation along the pain course, called **paresthesia**, which feels as though the affected area has gone to sleep. The pain is worse with bending, sneezing, coughing, and bearing down when defecating. There is tenderness of the back in the region of damage when the area is gently thumped with a fist.

Radicular back pain may come and go. If conservative therapy is followed—mild anti-inflammatory analgesics, bed rest, and physical therapy—many symptoms will be resolved. The probability of reinjury is great, however: about 50 percent.

Another chronic low back pain, usually associated with most other forms, is caused by *muscle spasm*. The muscles of the back may become strained or pulled by exercise, unhealthy back habits (picking up objects using the back muscles instead of the leg muscles), or by a variety of traumatic injuries.

Spasm is a reflex compensatory muscle action in the face of another back-related disorder. Pain from this disorder induces the response from the motor neuron to fire, which in turn contracts the muscle; prolonged contraction of the muscle stimulates pain receptors in the previously unaffected muscle. Even when the underlying causes of back pain are resolved, the spasm may persist.

Arthritis

Arthritis is an inflammation of the joints. Inflamed areas tend to ache constantly, with the pain being sharper when the joint is put in motion. The back is one long series of joints (between one vertebra and the next). It is persistently mobilized in each move that we make. Arthritis comes in several types.

Osteoarthritis, which comes as a consequence of aging and varies in its onset time, rate, and severity from one person to the next, is the most common form. It affects predominantly the vertebral column at all levels, the hips, and the knees and hands. It is also known as degenerative joint disease. In a sense, the disorder occurs in each of us as we grow older.

Rheumatoid arthritis is a much more severe disorder, which afflicts far fewer people but with greater severity. The inflammation can be in nearly any joint, but the hallmark is joint destruction. Severe damage and pain may require surgery to place artificial joints in the hands, knees, or hips or other restorative operations to improve joint function.

Other signs and symptoms of rheumatoid arthritis include muscle aches, morning stiffness, small nodules beneath the skin at select sites, fluid collections in the joint spaces, weakness, and blood-vessel narrowing in the fingertips upon exposure to cold, called Raynaud's phenomenon.

Lumbar stenosis refers to the narrowing of the spinal canal in the lower back region. The loss of space in the canal causes encroachment upon the spinal cord and its exiting nerves. This disorder usually arises from advanced osteoarthritis, predominantly in elderly persons. The pain is worst upon awakening or with extended walking, which is the opposite of a herniated disk.

Specific therapies for these disabling disorders include anti-inflammatory medications, pain medications, steroids, and medications containing gold.

Neck Pain Disorders

The same problems encountered in the lower back occur in the neck. *Muscle spasm* causes prolonged stiffness in the neck, with the added component of muscle tension headaches. The prolonged traction of the neck muscles on the lower part of the head is transmitted to the rest of the head muscles, thereby inducing a bandlike distribution of pain.

Radicular pain caused by herniated disks or advanced arthritis encroaches upon nerves that control the arm muscles and sensation. Manifest symptoms include local pain and radiated pain with paresthesias in the arm and hand, as well as focal and antalgic weakness.

Rheumatoid arthritis is more severe in the neck than in the lower spine. The joint destruction can cause one vertebra to slip out of line from the others. That process pinches not only the nearby nerves but also the spinal cord. The person so affected begins having urinary bladder control problems, spastic gait, and weakness in the legs and arms. The treatment of choice is usually surgical.

Cervical stenosis, or "shortening," is similar to lumbar stenosis, but it is more painful, and the signs are more like the vertebral changes of rheumatoid arthritis.

Thoracic outlet syndrome is a disorder that affects the major nerves of the neck. After they leave the vertebral column, the nerves pass through a region in the shoulder (the brachial plexus), where they intertwine with each other. If they become compressed—by neck muscles, lung tumors, blood vessel swellings called aneurysms, or metastatic breast cancer—the result is chronic pain, swelling, paresthesias, muscle wasting, and loss of arm function. Surgery and medications are frequently unsuccessful in relieving the symptoms.

Cranial Pain Syndromes

Headache is a widespread form of recurring disability. Many people just put up with it; others have their whole life altered by this episodic chronic pain disorder. One patient said she had quit law school and chosen another occupation based on the severity of her migraines, "the cross" she felt she had to bear. Successful therapy changed her whole life-style, once she finally sought medical care.

Headaches are of many definable types, but some kinds may occur simultaneously.

Muscle tension headaches are the most common form of headache. Sustained muscle contraction of the neck, shoulder, and temple results in a dull to mildly sharp pain that may be present upon awakening but typically worsens as the day and stresses continue. Relief comes from sleep, rest, aspirin, biofeedback, progressive muscle relaxation therapy, and antidepressant medications in low doses.

Migraine headaches in common parlance mean any severe head pain. Many persons refer to these headaches as "sinus" or "sick" headaches.

Migraines refer to headaches that are usually severe, with associated nausea. The blood vessels in the scalp dilate and make the scalp tender. Vomiting, sensitivity to light and sound, relief by sleep, and frequent relationship to alcohol use or the menstrual period are all characteristic associated features of common migraines.

Classical migraines include other focal neurological deficits at the first appearance of the headache, called the migrainous *aura.* Persons with these complain of visual changes before the pain onset that include bright shining or black spots, straight or zigzag lines, or loss of vision in half their visual field. Other patients may have additional deficits like weakened arm and leg, paresthesias, or inability to speak, which may last for minutes or even hours.

Cluster headaches are similar to migraines but are different enough to warrant another classification. Persons with these complain of periods during the year when a set of specific head pains cluster together. Usually there is a sharp unilateral pain centered behind the eye, radiating back to the ear and lasting for 20 to 60 minutes. Unilateral nasal stuffiness, red eye, and tearing are the hallmarks of cluster pain as is their predilection for nocturnal occurrence.

Whenever people have persistent headaches, they begin to wonder if they have a *brain tumor.* Most persons who suffer from the headaches already described know them as old friends. The occurrence of a different headache, or of a headache of increasing severity in someone without previous headaches, warrants suspicion of a tumor.

The headache associated with a brain tumor may be focal or generalized in its location of pain. Over time, the pain becomes progressively more frequent and severe.

Figure 8 provides a graphic comparison of these headaches.

FIGURE 8. Headache patterns

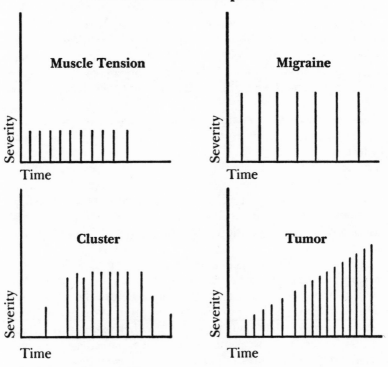

The most frequent severe facial pain of long duration is that of *trigeminal neuralgia (tic douloureux)*. The name comes from the nerve that supplies sensory information to the brain from the surface of the face, the cornea of the eye, and the oral cavity. The pain is sudden, lancinating, and lasts for less than thirty seconds. It occurs in volleys. As one woman reported, "The first time the pain struck, I just had to scream out!"—and she would have been considered stoic. The pain is typically triggered by specific pressure points on the face, smiling, eating, drinking, or brushing the teeth. The natural history is of waxing and waning severity with periods of relative quiescence.

Treatment is usually medical at first, using phenytoin (Dilantin) or carbamazepine (Tegretol), anticonvulsants used in **neuropathic** pain; baclofen (Lioresal); or standard analgesics. Surgical interventions—an x-ray guided injection of glycerol or cushioning the nerve where it passes next to the carotid artery—are helpful.

Atypical facial pain is a variant of trigeminal neuralgia. The symptoms are different enough to warrant a different diagnosis, but the treatment is essentially the same.

Thoracic or Chest Pain Syndromes

Angina pectoris, chest pain due to poor heart blood supply, is included in this section even though the pain is acute and relatively self-limited. The persistence of the episodic pain necessitates significant changes in life-style. The anxiety associated with a potentially life-threatening disorder becomes all-consuming to some persons afflicted with it.

The pain is described as a crushing pressure over the mid-chest. The patient usually symbolizes the pain with the universal sign of angina, the fisted hand over the central chest. Some say the pain is like an elephant sitting on your chest. The pain radiates to the left arm, neck, and side of the face to the level of the cheekbone, or it bores straight back to the shoulder blade. Nausea, profuse sweating, anxiety, agitation, light-headedness, and shortness of breath are frequent signs and symptoms. The pain typically comes upon exertion or emotional stress (but can occur at rest if the disease is far advanced), lasts less than thirty minutes, then resolves.

This disorder stems from narrowed blood vessels that supply blood to the heart. Atherosclerosis, or hardening of the arteries, causes the narrowing. When the demand for blood exceeds what the vessels can deliver, pain results. Treatment of angina is directed toward dilating the blood vessels by using nitrates or other agents that cause the vessels' muscular walls to relax.

Costal chondritis is inflammation of the chest wall cartilage. The symptoms include pain in the central chest region that is worse with movement of the chest wall but not necessarily associated with exercise. The pain may be reproduced by pressing on the chest wall, unlike the pain of angina pectoris. This disorder is frequently long-lasting and may be confused with angina by both patient and physician. It is treated with anti-inflammatory medications.

Abdominopelvic Pain Syndromes

Peptic ulcer disease is chronic inflammation and erosion of the tissues of the stomach wall. This also occurs in the duodenum, the first section of the small intestine into which the stomach dumps its contents. Duodenal ulcers account for 80 percent of all ulcers.

The causes for ulcers are many, especially oversecretion of stomach acid, hormonal changes, genetic predisposition, emotional and physical stress, and abnormalities of tissue resistance.

Inflammation of the bowel wall eventually sets off pain receptors located there. Erosion of the bowel follows in time. The worst outcome is when the bowel wall perforates, causing the contents of the intestine to leak into the peritoneum (the membrane that lines the abdominal cavity). This causes a chemical peritonitis, or inflamed peritoneum.

Symptoms of peptic ulcer include midabdominal (epigastric) pain that begins about two hours after a meal. The pain is usually a dull, burning sensation, often referred to as heartburn, but may be sharp enough to mimic anginal pain. The pain may also appear during the night, causing loss of sleep. Diarrhea, constipation, vomiting, and bleeding may accompany the pain.

If the patient doesn't follow the prescribed medication and dietary regimens, chronic pain will result. Peptic ulcer can change one's whole life.

Crohn's disease (regional enteritis or ileitis) is a lifelong disorder that stems from inflammation of a part of the gastrointestinal tract, usually the last section of the small bowel. Chronic pain in the right lower abdominal quadrant, associated with fever, weight loss, diarrhea, anorexia, nausea, and vomiting, characterizes this disease. Only 5 to 10 percent of patients die, but a great many are ill off and on throughout their lives. Multiple surgeries are usually required to remove bowel obstructions and kidney blockages and to repair draining fistulas, which are abnormal communications between two body organs or between an organ and the body surface.

Ulcerative colitis is similar to Crohn's disease but involves the large intestine. The signs and symptoms are of bloody diarrhea in great frequency during a day, weight loss, fever, and abdominal pain. These stem from an erosive ulceration of the large bowel wall, which leads to diffuse bleeding. Associated signs outside the colon include hepatitis, anemia, imbalance of electrolytes (essential minerals in the blood), arthritis, kidney stones, and skin changes. Also, there is a high proportion of cancer in connection with this disease.

Sickle cell anemia is a disorder caused by the genetically determined presence of hemoglobin S, found only in blacks. Hemoglobin is responsible for carrying oxygen in the red blood cells. Hemoglobin S is an inefficient carrier of oxygen, compared to the normal hemoglobin A, and its presence leads to inadequate tissue supply of oxygen. Patients may do well for an extended period until they go into sickle crisis: severe pain in the abdomen, joints, and chest, precipitated by extreme temperature change in the environment or concurrent infections. Treatment requires strong pain medications and, frequently, transfusions.

Endometriosis is a disorder caused by the extrauterine implantation of uterine cells. The peak age of occurrence is 30 to 40 years. Frequent signs and symptoms include pain during menstruation, interval bleeding or excessive menstrual bleeding, sterility, pain upon intercourse, low back pain, intermittent pelvic pain, and cyclic rectal bleeding. Treatment includes anti-inflammatory drugs, hormonal regulation, and the special medication danazol (Danacrine).

Pain Syndromes of the Extremities

Phantom limb pain is discussed in chapter 3.

Reflex sympathetic dystrophy is pain characterized by the excessive or abnormal response of the sympathetic nervous system to injury to the nerves, muscles, or blood vessels in the shoulder and arm or, rarely, just the arm. The protracted pain is associated with blue or ashen-colored skin in the affected limb and with swelling, coldness, and pain on passive motion. The affected bones become fragile. Another name for this is *shoulder–hand syndrome.* Sympathetic blockade, either pharmacologic or surgical, is the therapy of choice.

Causalgia is similar to reflex sympathetic dystrophy but comes from a partial injury to a major nerve in the arm or leg. There is an intense burning pain in the hand or foot that is most pronounced in the fingers or toes. The skin is moist, warm or cool, and becomes shiny, with scaly discoloration. Therapy is similar to that for reflex sympathetic dystrophy.

Neuropathic Pain

Neuropathy means, literally, suffering of the nerves. A *polyneuropathy* is a disorder of multiple nerves, usually in the peripheral nervous system. Systemic diseases like diabetes, hypothyroidism, and the presence of cancer in the body, particularly lung cancer, cause abnormalities in the conducting properties of the nerves. Intoxications or exposures to neurotoxins may lead to the same result. Usual toxins include prolonged alcohol abuse and mercury, arsenic, or lead poisoning. Syphilis or a deficiency of B vitamins may also cause a polyneuropathy.

Symptoms include poor sensation of the feet or hands, burning pain, shooting or lightning pain, pain upon walking (described as "walking on glass with bare feet"), and incoordination of balance (which makes walking even more difficult).

Treatment consists of eliminating the cause, such as treating the vitamin deficiency, clearing the syphilis infection, replacing the low thyroid hormone, withdrawing the alcohol, or removing the cancer. If these are ineffective, anticonvulsant agents like carbamazepine (Tegretol) and phenytoin (Dilantin) or antidepressant medications may relieve the symptoms. **Transcutaneous nerve stimulation** may be of help.

Postherpetic neuralgia is a painful aftereffect of herpes zoster viral infection (shingles). The patient usually has the typical skin eruption of small, circular, clear red bumps spread along the course of one or two nerves. The thoracic region is most frequently affected, but any nerve may be involved, including those in the face, arms, legs, mucous membranes, or eyes. This is a nonvenereally transmitted infection that has its highest incidence in persons on steroids or persons with cancer. Excruciating pain accompanies the disorder from the outset. The skin eruption resolves, as does the pain, usually in four weeks. But 7 to 33 percent of patients with the acute disorder continue to have pain for months or years later. Therapy requires steroids initially, followed by strong pain medications, anticonvulsants, and antidepressant/antipsychotic combinations.

Thalamic Pain Syndrome

As mentioned in chapter 3, a stroke in a particular part of the thalamus will cause it to begin transmitting pain messages on its own that are misinterpretations of normal stimuli. For example, the patient may say that the minimal sensation of an air draft across the arm feels as though a hot skillet had been applied to the area. Treatment consists of antidepressant medications, transcutaneous nerve stimulators, and **stereotactic surgery.**

Autoimmune Mediated Inflammatory Disorders

Each of us has a system within the body that is directed against any object or process that is deemed foreign. It basically identifies what is self and what is non-self. The system usually works to our benefit, affording us immunity to viruses, fighting bacteria, walling off foreign objects, and clearing debris from dying tissues.

In some individuals the ability to determine self is disordered, so that the immunity mechanisms are turned against both self and non-self. This is manifest by inflammatory reactions in otherwise normal tissues. Hence, this group of disorders is known as **autoim-**

mune inflammatory or collagen vascular disease, the primary targets being joints, connective tissue, and blood vessels.

Specific names of disorders in this category include rheumatoid arthritis, systemic lupus erythematosis, ankylosing spondylitis, polymyositis, polymyalgia rheumatica, and scleroderma. Each of these diseases has its own constellation of signs, in varying severity, the major ones being destructive arthritis, inflammation of the membranous coverings of the heart or lungs, blood vessel inflammation at varying sites, inflammation of muscles, and kidney damage.

Common symptoms include morning stiffness, joint pain, skin eruptions, reduced mobility, muscle pain, chest pain, hand pain upon exposure to cold temperature, and focal or generalized weakness.

Therapy includes salicylates, nonsteroidal anti-inflammatories, steroids, gold-containing medications, and nerve stimulators.

Pain Associated with Cancer

Abnormal growths in the body are divided into two types, benign and malignant. Benign lesions do not shorten the life expectancy of the person. They exert their ill effects from just enlarging in the area of origin (obstructing or compressing adjacent structures) and usually do not recur after total surgical removal. Malignant tumors shorten life expectancy, recur after complete removal, and exert more profound wide-ranging effects than local growth. Malignant tumors have the ability to appear at distant sites by a process known as *metastasizing*. The tumor at a distant site from the original is called a **metastasis**.

Chronic pain disorders related to cancers occur according to what the tumor does to the surrounding relatively normal tissue. Tumors themselves do not have pain sensation; the area around a tumor does. Should the tumor lie upon a nerve, the compression will cause pain fibers to be activated. If a bowel cancer grows to a size and position that obstructs the flow of materials passing through the region, the distention related to the obstruction causes pain. Metastases that affect the bone, as from lung and breast cancers, cause pain by weakening the bone and stimulating adjacent pain fibers.

So we may conclude that obstruction, compression, expansion in a limited space, and weakening of structural integrity are the general processes that cause a cancer patient to hurt.

Pain also comes as an unfortunate side effect of cancer therapy.

Chemotherapy causes abdominal or localized pain, with nausea, following administration of the medication. Surgery for removal of the tumor has its usual painful postoperative period. Chemotherapeutic agents can cause painful polyneuropathies.

Patients so afflicted present a major challenge. If the progress toward death cannot be slowed or averted, it is incumbent upon us to make the journey as comfortable as possible. Almost all therapies for chronic pain may be used in treating pain due to cancer. Varieties of the so-called **Brompton cocktail** developed by the British hospice movement are of great benefit for the cancer patient. This effective oral narcotic allows the patient to return home and live comfortably.

Psychiatric Causes of Chronic Pain

Many psychiatric conditions have associated bodily complaints. Whether a pain is "real" or not is a moot point from the patient's perspective. All pain is a perception. If the perception of pain is there, the pain exists.

From the physician's view, the point is not moot. The investigation of disorders that are only perceived and not caused by another underlying disorder (besides the psychiatric malady) opens up the possibility of *iatrogenic complications*—those caused by the physician. Just the process of investigating a complaint can cause significant disorders. On the other hand, the problem of dismissing a complaint as part and parcel of the psychiatric condition may lead to the neglect of a concurrent illness. What if the patient has two coexisting disorders that can cause pain, one psychiatric and the other structural?

An example of this dilemma is the overtly depressed person who complains of chronic low back pain that resulted from a job-related injury and is not helped by therapy. Does this person have a slipped disk, prostatic cancer, a benign spinal tumor, or a muscle spasm in that region? Or is the low back pain a manifestation of depression-related somatization, is it an example of a hysteroid personality, or is there significant secondary gain from not going to work while receiving disability payments? If an investigation shows equivocal findings, surgery may have major complications without relieving the primary problem. Or, if not investigated, a concurrent illness may be overlooked that might have been treated with good results while the psychiatric disease was addressed.

The disorders in this category are more amply covered in chapter 2 by Wayne Oates. They are listed here for completion:

Depression with somatization disorder or amplification of preexisting pain

Hysterical personality

Briquet's syndrome

Malingering

Munchausen's syndrome

5

Pain Therapy
and Management

As a pastor, you are an integral part of the treatment team, because you have a unique relationship with the patient. The physician, nurse, psychologist, physical therapist, and pharmacist usually lose contact with the patient upon discharge from the hospital or outpatient clinic. You, the pastor, see the person as an in-patient parishioner with medical problems, but you also see the person at home, at church, and elsewhere in daily life. You are part of that daily life. Through your encouragement and instruction as an informed pastor, the parishioner may continue pain treatment.

Every interaction with a pain patient has the potential for being either therapeutic or countertherapeutic. You have the opportunity to continue teaching patients who are at home about their disease and its therapy; to monitor signs of maladaptive behavior, medication use and abuse, reinforcement of non–pain behavior, and reduction of anxiety by ventilation for anxiety reduction; and to guide these patients as a pastoral counselor.

With the parishioner's permission, you may report developments to the attending physician. The physician usually must rely on observations by patients and family members that may be biased and subjective. As a pastor, you have an advantage, for you are able to observe directly in many roles and environments. For this reason, your knowledge of pain therapy (and its shortcomings) will be most valuable in understanding the process and outcome of treatment.

General Considerations of Pain Therapy

After a new patient has been interviewed and examined, the physician tries to categorize the disorder(s) present and refer in mind or text to the prescribed therapies. Unfortunately, when there is little confirmable evidence, as is often the case in chronic pain, there are many opinions as to what needs to be done.

The next question is whether more diagnostic investigation is needed or whether the patient is simply in need of relief from pain.

Finally, the treatment most likely to be successful must be chosen. Pharmacologic, surgical, noninvasive, or combined therapies are possible.

It is rare for different physicians to recommend exactly the same treatment. Multiple combinations may be effective where individually each failed, and some combinations may work for one patient but fail in others with the same disorder.

Pharmacologic Therapy

The following discussion refers to the various drugs used to treat pain by their class and generic names, but not always by proprietary names. For further examples of proprietary drugs in each class, please refer to the Appendix of Drug Names at the back of the book.

Salicylates. Salicylates are commonly available drugs, best represented by aspirin. Their action is analgesic, antipyretic (fever-reducing), mildly blood-thinning, and anti-inflammatory. These medications work by inhibiting the synthesis of **prostaglandin**, a naturally occurring compound in the body that mediates blood vessel dilation, inflammation and pain caused by tissue trauma, and the hypothalamic response in temperature regulation.

This class of medications is effective for mild to moderate pain and is available without prescription. The strength is about one tenth that of codeine in equal milligram doses.

Salicylates are indicated in disorders like arthritis that are accompanied by inflammation of all types. They work well with muscle tension headaches. They are good in combination with pain therapies that lack anti-inflammatory effects.

Side effects include heartburn, gastrointestinal bleeding, nausea, and vomiting.

Toxic effects at prolonged high doses include kidney damage, propensity for bleeding, liver damage, and coma. Symptoms of toxicity include nausea, vomiting, ringing in the ears (tinnitus), mental confusion, and rapid breathing.

Drug allergy manifest by rash, shortness of breath, or itching is not uncommon and is, as for any other medication listed here, an indication that the drug should be discontinued.

Acetaminophen. Acetaminophen is used in place of salicylate in those persons with a known allergy or intolerance to aspirin. It has the analgesic and antipyretic properties of aspirin but lacks the latter's anti-inflammatory and blood-thinning properties. Acetaminophen is effective in the same disorders treated by salicylates but will not address any underlying inflammation, which may be significant in many painful conditions. This drug may be effective in mild to moderate pain. When used in conjunction with other agents, the combined effect may be significant.

Toxic manifestations of acetaminophen include blood abnormalities, liver destruction, and kidney damage.

Steroids. Steroids are natural or man-made compounds that slow or stop the process of inflammation. Steroids are not considered an analgesic but are included here because they reduce swelling and inflammation, which in turn relieves pain. They are naturally produced by adrenal gland as a type of hormone. Their effects are many and wide-ranging.

Steroids preparations are used to treat a wide variety of painful disorders, specifically rheumatoid arthritis and the other autoimmune disorders, post and acute herpetic neuralgia, migraines, regional enteritis, and ulcerative colitis.

Side effects include weight gain, fluid retention, bone demineralization, peptic ulcers, gastrointestinal bleeding, among others. Toxicity is manifested by heart failure, mental derangements such as psychosis, convulsions, and further worsening of the listed side effects. Consequently, steroids are used sparingly.

Nonsteroidal anti-inflammatories. Nonsteroidal anti-inflammatory medications are more characteristic of the salicylates in their action of prostaglandin synthesis. They also reduce inflammation and are analgesic in that capacity. This group of drugs has rapidly expanded during the last decade, for they are effective in treating the same disorders as the salicylates without as significant gastrointestinal upset and hemorrhage. The side effects are similar to the salicylates, but congestive heart failure is also a possibility. Examples of these medications are ibuprofen (Motrin), now sold over the counter, naproxen (Naprosyn), and indomethacin (Indocin).

Antidepressants. The chronic pain patient may suffer from depression, either additionally or as a result of the persistent pain. That depression deserves treating. No matter what the disorder, depression makes it worse.

Antidepressants work by replenishing the central nervous system's supply of such neurotransmitters as serotonin and norepinephrine. We saw in chapter 3 that serotonin is necessary for the patient's own opiate system to be effective and to help mediate the gate mechanism of pain control. The increase of serotonin helps *both* the depression *and* the body's normal built-in way of controlling pain.

Antidepressants are used in chronic pain states, either alone or with other medications. They work best in treating **neuropathic** pain and low back pain. They are also helpful in sleep disorders related to pain.

Side effects include dry mouth, light-headedness, blurred vision, constipation, and sedation.

Toxicity is a severe problem with any depressed person, for the possibility of an intentional overdose is always present. Toxic levels of antidepressants produce coma, respiratory depression, and heart rhythm disturbances, all of which are life-threatening.

Major Tranquilizers (Antipsychotics). Antipsychotics are frequently used with antidepressants in restoring the correct neurotransmitter balance in the central nervous system, because of their additive effect. Examples are chlorpromazine (Thorazine) and haloperidol (Haldol). Their side effects are similar to the antidepressants.

This group of medications may induce a dose-related side effect similar to the rigidity of Parkinson's disease: acute *dystonia,* an involuntary stiff, contorted posture of the face, mouth, and/or limbs, separately or in combination. The eyes may be similarly affected; for minutes or hours, the eyeballs stick in one position (called an *oculogyric crisis*).

Another toxic reaction is known as *akathisia,* which comes from the Greek and means "without sitting down." The patient complains of a very annoying inner restlessness and paces back and forth. These drugs may also cause damage to the skin and the liver.

After moderate to prolonged use, antipsychotics may induce involuntary movements of the face and mouth, called *tardive dyskinesia,* which appear as a constant chewing movement, with varying amounts of tongue protrusion. Even when the medication is stopped, the movements may continue for weeks, months, or years. There is no therapy for these late-appearing involuntary movements, so these medications *should not be given on a permanent basis.*

Minor Tranquilizers (Anxiolytics). Anxiolytics are used to reduce the anxiety that is part and parcel of suffering with pain. They work at the level of the limbic system. Examples of these drugs are diazepam (Valium), chlordiazepoxide (Librium), and lorazepam (Ativan).

Another benefit of these drugs, not related to anxiety, is their effect at the spinal-cord level to induce muscular relaxation. Remember that the vicious cycle of pain → muscle contraction → pain discussed in chapter 3 is self-perpetuating, causing pain irrespective of the original insult. Anxiolytic medications work to break that cycle.

Side effects include sedation, fatigue, and staggering gait. Toxicity is manifested by respiratory depression and impaired consciousness. Abrupt withdrawal after prolonged usage may induce nausea, vomiting, sweating, and convulsions. Psychologic dependence is more probable than physiologic dependence with these drugs.

Anticonvulsants

Anticonvulsant drugs are used primarily in the treatment of epilepsy and other seizure disorders. Some are used for chronic pain, usually of the neuropathic type. This does not mean the patient has epilepsy; rather, the mechanism of action works on both peripheral nerves and the central nervous system. Examples of anticonvulsants are phenytoin (Dilantin), carbamazepine (Tegretol), and valproate (Depakene).

These medications are indicated for use in peripheral neuropathies, trigeminal neuralgia, postherpetic neuralgia, some forms of chronic low back pain, and some types of headache. Their action in these disorders is unclear, but since their chemical structure is close to antidepressant medication, they probably work by means of altering neurotransmitters related to pain.

Side effects include nausea, vomiting, sedation, and light-headedness.

Toxicity is manifest by worsening of the above side effects, along with slurred speech, staggering gait, and altered level of consciousness.

Narcotic Analgesics

The premier narcotic analgesic is morphine. All other drugs are measured by morphine's superior analgesia. The other drugs of this group are the same as morphine when given in equivalent dosage. They work by stimulating the opiate receptors (see chapter 3).

Narcotics are meant to be used in acute pain disorders and somewhat sparingly in chronic pain disorders. Their efficacy is markedly diminished when given orally instead of parenterally—that is, by vein or intramuscularly—which makes using them outside the hospital difficult but not impossible.

Side effects of morphine are sedation, euphoria, dysphoria, constipation, nausea, sweating, light-headedness, and disorientation.

Toxic manifestations include respiratory depression, coma, severe blood pressure drop (hypotension), and hallucinations.

The **Brompton cocktail**, a combination of morphine with other agents in elixir form, deserves comment. Used for severe chronic pain usually associated with cancer, it is a liquid oral medication that contains varying combinations of morphine, cocaine, a major tranquilizer, alcohol, chloroform water, and a flavoring syrup. Each component has an additive effect in treating the pain disorder, but their side effects counteract one another. Cocaine induces euphoria and is a stimulant that counteracts the sedative and dysphoric qualities of the morphine. The alcohol and tranquilizers work to increase analgesia and decrease the psychic components. The chloroform water is a preservative, and the syrup improves the taste of the mixture. Present-day clinical use varies the ingredients and dosages.

This medication is convenient for both patient and family, for it may be administered relatively easily and has good efficacy. A variation is used in behaviorally oriented chronic pain treatment centers and for pain-ridden cancer patients.

Addiction and Pain

Those who have chronic pain usually show a continuing sense of desperation. Escape from that desperation is a golden ring at which to grasp. Strong pain medications offer that golden ring each time they are given. Also, narcotics are rewarding in and of themselves.

These two components are the basis for what is referred to as *psychologic dependence.* First, the relief of desperation, anxiety, and depression and a return to normalcy appeals to anyone who suffers. Respondent conditioning occurs because of the euphoria and sedation caused by some medications. Eventually the behavior becomes operantly conditioned, because the other benefits of the medicated "fog" begin to have a reward; that is, drugs may be used as a form of illegal tender. Both characteristics drive what is known as *drug-seeking behavior.*

Physiologic dependence refers to those physical signs and symptoms that appear upon abrupt discontinuance of a medication. When a person with physiologic dependence stops taking a narcotic cold turkey, an agitation and craving for the medication begins within hours to days. Associated symptoms include abdominal pain, palpitations, insomnia, headache, and nausea. Signs include sweating, salivation, and increased heart rate, blood pressure, respiratory rate, and pupillary size. This constellation of signs and symptoms constitutes the *abstinence syndrome*. This state gradually wanes if the person continues for 2 to 7 days without the addictive drug. Should the person restart the drug, the symptoms abate in moments to hours.

A person may be called addicted to a drug, but that does not necessarily mean that both physiologic and psychologic dependence are present. It is possible for a person to be physically dependent on a drug without being psychologically dependent. Or a person may be psychologically dependent without physical addiction. A person who becomes physically dependent on a narcotic after three weeks of therapy for a fractured pelvis is not psychologically dependent, while a person with a compulsive neurosis may become psychologically dependent on, say, Valium without manifesting physical dependence when the medication is discontinued.

This description of the abstinence syndrome refers mostly to narcotics. Yet the pain patient may become addicted to many other drugs. Alcohol is a prime candidate because it relieves pain and anxiety while relaxing the muscles. People rarely die from untreated acute narcotic withdrawal, whereas an abrupt withdrawal from the heavy consumption of alcohol may cause profound delirium and convulsions and has an untreated mortality rate of 14 percent!

Who is prone to significant withdrawal signs and symptoms if alcohol consumption is stopped? Published figures do not provide a very understandable clinical criterion for determining an individual's risk. My personal experience in treating scores of inner-city patients is this: The half-pint-per-day patient marks the beginning of those who will experience problems with withdrawal, and at a pint of whiskey per day the probability increases exponentially.

One last note on withdrawal from alcohol: The syndrome is not an all-or-nothing phenomenon. Symptoms and signs may be as subtle as mildly increased heart rate and blood pressure.

Misconceptions Concerning Pharmacologic Pain Management

Considerable bias is present in the way a physician orders medications. There is as much belief and personal philosophy associated with dispensing medication as there is sound pharmacologic background. As a result there are many misconceptions about pain medications.

The average university-based physician undertreats pain with analgesic medications. One study showed that, given a patient who was suffering an acute heart attack, all physicians felt that total pain relief was indicated. But when they ordered the narcotic, 72 percent ordered doses that were two thirds or less of what was indicated for that pain relief, and the medication was given every four hours instead of on the every-three-hour schedule dictated by duration of the drug action.

Though the placebo effect is a real advantage in improving a medication's analgesic efficacy, the average physician uses it most consciously when trying to determine if a pain is "real" or "psychogenic," and especially for difficult or problem patients. These persons are least apt to respond to a placebo.

Pain medications are usually administered on a p.r.n. or "as needed" basis. Patients must ask for the medication to receive relief. They must present pain behaviors in order to be rewarded by pain reduction and medication benefit. This is a paradigm for creating operant pain, and it happens every day of a pain patient's existence. Operant pain persists beyond the cessation of nociception, yet the patient's environment is instrumental in developing it.

Analgesics are less effective in reducing preexistent unabated pain than in preventing the rise of pain. Often patients wait until they cannot stand any more suffering before taking an analgesic, perhaps out of stoicism or the fear of being a junkie. Yet if the medication is used before the pain gets bad, the drug is more effective and the overall total dose is less.

The period between doses of narcotic medications has a peak and a trough. Just after a dose, the patient is "snowed" and is likely to sleep. Just before the next dose, most of the medication has worn off so the patient begins experiencing pain. Toward the middle of the descent from peak to trough, the patient starts to develop anxiety about the pain to come in the trough. More pain-related behavior occurs, for anxiety increases pain.

The constant infusion of medication by vein avoids this cycle of pain followed by sedation. Alternatively, a small portable pump connected to a needle placed under the skin keeps the blood level of the medication constant while allowing the patient to move around.

Many of the problems just mentioned arise because the physician has incomplete information, has unfounded fears of causing addiction, and, in some cases, believes that analgesics are to be avoided at all costs.

To summarize, pain medications should be given on a regular

basis that corresponds to their duration of action. "As needed" regimens induce operant pain. Doses should be quantitatively based on the patient's weight and size and should be scheduled before need, not in catch-up doses.

Surgical Therapy for Pain

The therapy a patient receives for a given pain is directly related to the speciality of the physician who is consulted. An internist will probably récommend medication. A surgeon will be more likely to recommend surgery, if the disorder is amenable to a surgical procedure. The trouble with surgery is that after something has been done, one cannot return to the untreated state to start over again. And surgery is more likely to yield unwanted permanent side effects than is medication alone.

This is the basis of the algorithm for pain management. The patient's medical management for intractable pain must have thoroughly failed before surgery is contemplated. The more invasive the treatment, the more permanent the outcome and the later it should come in the process of pain treatment. Pain disorders for which a known surgical therapy is the first choice and pain in a patient with a short life expectancy, usually caused by a malignant cancer, are exceptions to this principle.

Figure 9 shows where specific surgeries interrupt the pain pathway.

Nerve Blocks

An area of pain may be in the distribution of a single nerve, such as the trigeminal nerve, related to trigeminal neuralgia. Direct injection of the nerve with a blocking agent like xylocaine temporarily stops information from being carried along that nerve. After the xylocaine wears off, the nerve can once again send pain messages to the central nervous system. This process allows the attending physician to see if the pain resolves when the block is present and, if so, if a more long-lasting or permanent block would be beneficial.

The action of blocking agents is of varying duration. Long-lasting blocking agents may interrupt the cycle of pain by stopping the pain transmission that stimulates the muscle into spasm.

Somc blocking agents are **neurolytic**, which means that they kill the injected nerve. Before such a permanent block is administered, a short-acting block is tried.

Injections into the area just outside the spinal cord, called the

FIGURE 9. Surgical therapy for pain

 Region of stimulation-produced anesthesia

 Area of stereotactic ablation

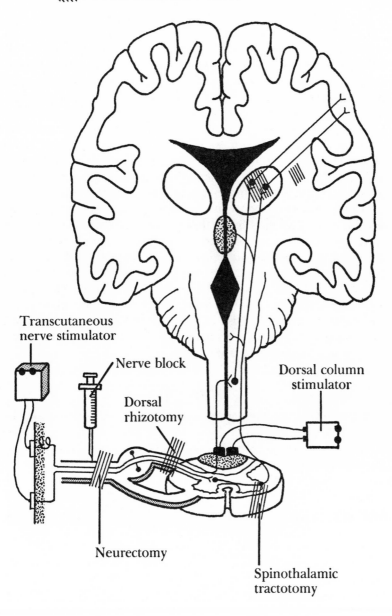

epidural space, are done using morphine, steroids, or blocking agents. This applies the different medications at the source where active pain neurons are discharging. You will recall that the spinal cord and nerve root pass through that region, so that anti-inflammatories and opiate receptor stimulation would be effective.

Neurotomy and Tractotomy

Both the neurotomy and the tractotomy procedures involve the cutting of nerves, as the suffix "-otomy" implies. *Neurotomy,* the cutting of a peripheral nerve, will stop the pain information for weeks to months. The nerve will grow back at a rate of 1mm per day until it finally reconnects with its receptors.

Some nerves do not grow back to their receptors but grow into a knot at the remnant stump. The knot is called a *neuroma,* which may lead to the spontaneous firing of pain sensation information when none is received from the environment. Neuromas may occur after trauma or other unintentional injury to a nerve.

Tractotomy is the surgical cutting of a pain fiber tract in the spinal cord. We saw in chapter 3 that the anterolateral spinothalamic tract, lying just on the outer surface of the spinal cord, conducts pain information toward the thalamus and brain stem (the neospinal and paleospinal pathways). Cutting this tract prevents most of the pain messages from the contralateral body segment from reaching the higher central nervous system. But some fibers do not cross to the contralateral tract; they rise in the ipsilateral spinothalamic tract. These ipsilateral fibers are thought to be why postoperative pain returns in six months to two years.

Rhizotomy

Rhizotomy is the surgical cutting of the dorsal root just outside the spinal cord. This cuts the axon just before its entry into the dorsal horn. The cut pain fiber is thereby prevented from connecting with the next neuron in the pain pathway.

Rhizotomy is indicated in conditions of severe pain arising from regions supplied by one or two nerve trunks, each of which receives information from several individual peripheral nerves.

Intracranial Surgery

The process by which a neurosurgeon burns very minute areas deep in the middle of the brain that are related to pain processing is called **stereotactic surgery**. By using physical landmarks apparent on x-rays, computer calculations, and a special targeting harness applied to the patient's head, the neurosurgeon is able to place a long thin electrode into the patient's brain with little disruption of unrelated structures. When the electrode reaches the proper area, an x-ray is taken showing its position in the skull. Next, the neurosurgeon either cools or electrically stimulates a region (such as the thalamus) to see if the change in the area correlates with the desired effect. The patient is able to respond to questions concerning sensation and function, for the surgery is performed under local anesthesia with the patient awake. Paradoxically, the brain feels no pain.

In other areas of pain, surgery in the brain is performed under direct visualization. *Cingulotomy* refers to the cutting of nerve fibers in the cingulum, a structure in the limbic system. This surgery alters the patient's subconscious processing of pain so that pain is not perceived as noxious.

Prefrontal lobotomy destroys the nerve fibers that connect the frontal lobes to other regions of the brain, thus interrupting the processing of nociception. It was once used in intractable schizophrenia. As a more refined technique, it has a limited application in intractable pain. The major drawback associated with this operation is the significant personality change after its completion.

Intractable bone pain associated with metastatic breast or prostate cancer is occasionally treated by hypophysectomy, which is the removal of the pituitary gland (also known as the hypophysis). This gland is situated on the underside of the frontal lobes behind the nasal passages and is approached surgically through the sinuses.

Although the anterior pituitary produces beta endorphins, the pain relief is not mediated by this mechanism but, rather, is felt to be due to hormonal alteration.

The postoperative problems associated with maintaining life without the pituitary gland are great, and this procedure is best used in patients with intractable pain and a short life expectancy.

Stimulation-Produced Analgesia (SPA)

Electrical stimulation of deep brain structures may be accomplished by stereotactic implantation of small electrodes. When the periaqueductal gray region of the brain stem is mildly stimulated electrically, analgesia is produced that lasts for hours beyond the short stimulation period. The person is able to function normally because the implanted stimulation devices are controlled by radio frequency from external transmitting devices. Stimulation on a two-to three-times-per-day basis is enough to relieve the protopathic pain mediated by that region. The stimulation is correlated with increased spinal-fluid levels of endorphins.

This area of treatment may develop in the future, but it is still highly experimental.

Dorsal Column Stimulation

As described in chapter 3, the spinal-cord dorsal columns receive considerable input from ipsilateral A-delta fibers. The tract of fibers eventually connects with the contralateral thalamus. This system modulates pain at the spinal-cord level by the gating mechanism and by altering thalamic pain processing. Direct electrical stimulation of the dorsal columns has the effect of decreasing the intensity and frequency of pain signals at the spinal-cord level. The stimulator is implanted under x-ray guidance by a neurosurgeon. Placement requires only a small skin incision; therefore, this is not a major operation. The stimulator may be removed or permanently incorporated, depending on the benefit imparted.

Nonpharmacologic and Nonsurgical Therapy

This category of pain management is composed of interventions that are adjuncts to those already described. Most chronic pain patients receive a combination of treatments. Few are mutually exclusive. Indeed, multiple treatment types are at times synergistic— that is, they work together and their combined effect is greater than the sum of their parts.

The following treatments may work well enough alone, but chronic pain is usually treated more effectively by several modalities at once.

Transcutaneous Nerve Stimulation (TNS)

Transcutaneous nerve stimulation is the noninvasive equivalent of the dorsal column stimulation already described. The device used is a small battery-operated appliance that looks like a transistor radio and is worn on a belt. Two to four electrode wires run from the TNS unit to electrode pads, similar to electrocardiogram patches, placed on the skin in the region of pain and arranged by the patient. Upon the appliance are knobs that vary the stimulus intensity, frequency, and duration. These are adjusted by the patient until the correct combination of settings is found.

The TNS unit stimulates the A-delta fibers, which impart presynaptic inhibition of C fibers. This is the gate theory of pain control. In chronic pain syndromes, endorphins in the spinal fluid are depressed; transcutaneous nerve stimulation causes a rise in the endorphin level. This rise of endorphins and the effect of the TNS is blocked by naloxone.

A major use of TNS units has been in low back pain, muscle tension headaches, and polyneuropathies.

Pain patients often feel helpless to improve their own condition. The TNS unit provides something *patients* can do to alter the pain. Efficacy of the TNS unit is aided by the placebo effect and the reduction of anxiety on the part of the patient, but it is not dependent solely on them.

Acupuncture

Much research has followed the introduction of this ancient Oriental therapy into Occidental medicine, but as yet not all the answers are in concerning either mechanism or efficacy.

The ancient prescientific theory is based on cosmic energy known as *chi*, which is composed of positive and negative forces that are balanced in the manner of the *yin* and *yang*. The forces are aligned in meridians of the body. Along the meridians, points are present that correspond to specific organ systems. Tapered needles are inserted into the skin at these points and are rotated. This induces a deep ache in the muscle called *teh chi*. After stimulation, the needle is removed. The pain relief imparted may last hours to weeks beyond the therapy session.

Modern theory sees the gate theory of pain control as the primary action of acupuncture. The effect is endorphin-mediated, for the analgesia is blocked when naloxone is administered at the same time.

Acupuncture has been shown to be effective for certain patients with acute pain disorders. Patient selection is important, for successful treatment requires cooperation and suggestibility on the part of the patient. The role of acupuncture in chronic pain is less clear, but anecdotal evidence suggests poor results.

Systematic Muscle Relaxation

Systematic muscle relaxation has been effectively used in many pain, stress, and anxiety-producing states. The program is easily learned and taught to both patients and allied health professionals.

The interested pastor may well learn and use this technique (see chapter 7).

The mechanism of this therapy has roots in the pain → muscle spasm → pain cycle. Relaxation of the muscles helps reduce anxiety and stress and also helps reduce the autogenic stimulation of muscle pain receptors.

The patient must use this technique on a regular basis and also as a response to increased pain. A regular basis has to be maintained, just like taking medications; hit-and-miss therapy has hit-and-miss results. This point cannot be overemphasized.

Biofeedback

Like relaxation training, biofeedback involves patients in actively doing something about their pain. They are able to gain some control of the uncontrollable by altering a physiologic parameter.

The procedure is related specifically to the area and the nature of the patient's problem. For example, the resting activity of the neck muscles is what perpetuates a muscle tension headache. Therefore, the patient is enabled to see and hear that activity by placing electrode patches over the neck muscles, which are connected to an amplifier and then to a television screen. When there is elevated resting activity in the muscles, the patient sees a coarse jagged line on the screen and hears a loud roaring from the amplifier. It is up to the patient, with teaching from the therapist, to reduce the visual and auditory display to baseline, which correlates with relaxed muscles in the region of the electrodes. In technical terms, the patient is operantly conditioned by the therapist and the machinery for actions that reduce muscle tension. Relaxed muscles lead to fewer headaches, which is inherently reinforcing.

This method is useful in treating headaches, low back pain, and anxiety, but it requires technology, good cooperation, and practice on the part of the patient.

Hypnosis

Hypnosis, as led by the therapist and eventually done alone by the patient, has the ability to induce a trancelike state that displaces the pain from consciousness. The trance helps to dissociate the pain from the present while distorting the sense of time: a useful device, because severe pain seems to go on for a millennium. This interferes with the perception of pain when the frequency of the pain signal increases.

The basic strategy also relies on blocking pain through direct suggestion. The mental image of the pain is displaced from one large area to a correspondingly smaller one. The pain is reinterpreted to mean something different and less noxious.

Psychotherapy

Psychotherapy is useful in the ventilation of anxiety and fears by both patient and family. It is useful in helping patients make life-style changes that lead to a more serene outlook. Psychotherapy is also useful as a way of positively reinforcing behavior that relieves the pain and of providing hope for depressed and anxious pain patients. Interpretive therapy helps the patient put the malady of pain in perspective. Also, it redirects the patient toward untapped strengths available for pain control. Cognitive strategies for mental displacement and control of pain may be taught to more sophisticated patients. Antidepressant and anxiolytic medications may be overseen by the psychiatrist as needed for the depression attendant in chronic pain.

Behavioral Therapy and the Chronic Pain Unit

Operant pain involves a set of pain-related behaviors that include talking about the pain, seeking medical attention, expecting reductions in work responsibilities, and interacting with other persons in the environment who reinforce the sick role.

Behavioral therapy for chronic pain is directed at decreasing these behaviors. The behavioral therapist directs attention toward what patients do and not what they say about their pain. For example, a patient may report severe low back pain and yet be able to play a set of tennis. The activity of tennis, or "up time," is the measure, not the self-report, for self-report is the dependent variable to a multitude of independent variables that may or may not be related to nociception.

A chronic pain therapy management unit is designed to increase "up time," that time when the pain patient participates in normal daily activities. This and reducing medication use are the cardinal parameters for determining success.

The pain unit is a physical structure or area where a multispecialty team works for about four weeks with each pain patient. The team is composed of physicians (orthopedists, neurologists, anesthesiologists, and/or physiatrists), nurse clinicians, nursing staff, physical and occupational therapists, dieticians, pharmacists, and recreational therapists. All these specialists coordinate their skills at assessing the individual's needs, environmental reinforcers of pain behavior, and family setting. By ignoring the pain behavior while reinforcing any non-pain behavior, the team mobilizes the pain patient into more "up time." Chaplains are becoming increasingly involved and are implementing resources of faith in these pain units.

When the patient arrives at the unit, several days of baseline medication usage, sleep and activity schedule, and diagnostic evaluations are undertaken. The baseline medication usage determines the medication reduction schedule to be used.

Each patient in the unit receives a liquid oral analgesic much like the Brompton cocktail described earlier. The baseline requirement of medication is initially included in the cocktail and given at fixed intervals. Over the treatment month, the analgesic is systematically reduced. The patient knows this is occurring but is unaware of *when* the dose is reduced, for the cocktail always has the same taste and volume.

Physical therapy, structured recreational activities, group psychotherapy and teaching sessions, and diagnostic investigations fill the average patient's day.

Families are taught behavior modification skills and physical therapy maneuvers or exercises and are encouraged to be part of the treatment program. The family and the patient are ultimately responsible for carrying on after the patient is discharged.

This protocol for treatment of chronic pain is not uniformly applicable to every patient. Behavior modification requires considerable motivation and cooperation on the part of both patient and family. A quarter of the patients drop out of the program, and these persons are fairly vocal about their discontent. At best, the six-month follow-up shows about 50 percent improvement over baseline. Patients who are poorly compliant, angry, and demanding of perfection from any therapy tried are not suited for this form of pain management.

Whether the treatment succeeds or fails after discharge depends chiefly on compliance with the program. Outpatient "tuning" of the learned behaviors could be of great benefit. You, as pastor, can do much to reinforce good results in aftercare.

We come to the end of our crash course in the physiology and pathology of pain. Pain is a "friendly enemy," a friend protecting us from danger, but one who may stay too long and become a hindrance instead of a help. You as a pastor are often at life's crossroads for people in pain. They may have had a severe and acute encounter and come to your attention in this crisis. Then, as the acute pain subsides, they are at risk of having chronic pain become a way of life. You are with them then as their spiritual director. You see them at church, in the shopping districts, on parent-teacher days at school, and in many other places. You have the privilege of visiting as a welcome guest in their homes and of expressing pastoral concern about their well-being.

Therefore, none of our crash course need be forgotten. You can use it in helping persons decide to get medical assistance and in making referrals. You can use it in helping them to comply with the regimens of exercise, meditation, muscular relaxation, and medication and many of the means of care set up by the team of pain treatment experts, of which you are a vital part. You can effectively inspire many pain patients to move from a passive response to their condition to an active one. The more knowledgeable you are, the more specific you can make the good news of God in these respects for them. As pastor, you can be a physician of pain *behaviors*, whereas the physician is the pastor of pain physiology, pathology, and medication. You can reread these chapters and be a *fisicien*, the Old French word for one knowledgeable in medical arts. For indeed you are a "physician of the soul," which in my spiritual education means the physician of the whole life of your people.

6

The Perception
of Pain

Having searched out the physiology of pain, the most common forms and syndromes of pain, and the varieties of medical intervention for pain, we need now to explore the meaning of pain for patients in the context of the personal and social world in which they live. Meaning forms in the mind of the pain patient as it does with anyone else: through perception.

Plato, Aristotle, Augustine, and many others over the centuries have thought of pain as the opposite of pleasure. It has been described as a "passion of the soul." As Augustine says, "But pain in the flesh is only a discomfort of the soul arising from the flesh, and a kind of shrinking from its suffering" (*The City of God*, XIV, 14–15). This popular idea still exists. However, the scientific study of pain has altered our understanding. As psychology professor Frank A. Goddard says, pain has come to be thought of "as an independent member of the family of cutaneous senses" (p. 317).

Some psychologists in the last century thought of perception as a compounding of sensory images, particularly visual ones, with the mental set of a person's nervous predisposition, muscular responses, associations from previous learning, and the particular environmental events happening at the time pain is felt. Gestalt psychologists approached perception differently. Take pain, for example. According to the Gestalt psychologists, you and I experience pain immediately in terms of a whole pattern of meaning. We perceptually grasp *as a totality,* and not as a collection of elements, what a given aching, wrenching, or stabbing pain means in our consciousness. This meaning must then be checked, verified, or modified as we live with the pain. Our "private meaning" may or may not be accurate.

David Bakan rightly observes that pain is a private, lonely experience (p. 61). "Pain is ultimately private in that it is lodged in the individual person. . . . Another paradox is that a cry of pain coming from one person may evoke in another an effort to help the person who is in pain; and thus pain is also a means of returning to the dominion of the social telos." Herein, then, is the crux of the pastoral care of pain patients: that we suspend our own judgments about the validity or lack of validity of their perception of pain; that we respond to their cry for help by entering *their* world as they perceive it; that we join with them in seeking and collecting all data that can be known about the sources and nature of their pain; that we build a life support community around them to help in bearing and modifying their pain; that the fellowship of learning itself will change beneficially both their perception of pain and the pain itself; and that we do all these things as servants of Jesus Christ and in his name.

The Mechanisms of the Perception of Pain

How do persons perceive pain? We must be cautious in our answers to this question. Jean Piaget warns us that "a psychological entity is always in danger of being overthrown by the discovery of a correct neurological explanation" (p. xxi). We are collaborating here, as pastoral counselor and neurologist, to offset this possibility.

The Absence of Pain

Pain has positive functions: it helps us withdraw from such harmful agents as fire, extreme cold, and such instruments as sharp knives and it serves as a warning system for diseases and dysfunctions of the body.

A small number of people, sixty-five at least, have been reported who were born without the ability to perceive pain. They may survive, but the risk of neglecting such things as burns, fractures, and infections is extremely high, and these persons have much shorter lives as a result.

The perception of pain is lessened when high rewards for bearing the pain are present. Soldiers wounded severely at Anzio Beach were less aware of pain than a similarly damaged group of civilians. Their previous discipline in hardship, combined with their relief at being alive but wounded and eligible to stop fighting, made them less perceptive of severe pain. Football players, too, are reported as "playing with pain"; that is, ignoring injury in the excitement of competition (Beecher, 1946).

The Effects of Placebo

"Placebo" is a Latin word meaning "I shall please." In English use as a medical term, a placebo is an inactive substance or procedure used in research studies or treatment in contrast to active medicines to rule out the possibility that the medication is only psychologically affecting the patient's perception of pain. Often one group of patients is given the inactive substance and another an active medication, with neither patient nor physician knowing what the patient is receiving, active or placebo medication. Then results from the two groups are compared. These are called "double blind" studies. "In 13 double blind studies an average of 36% achieved significant relief from pain after ingesting a placebo" (Evans, pp. 289–290). However, these were persons who were subjected to artificially and experimentally induced pain. Other studies of post-operative pain found that morphine provided a 52 percent pain relief factor and placebos recorded a 40 percent relief factor.

Jerome Frank attributes the placebo effect to the way it "mobilizes the patient's expectancy of help," to "its symbolic power," and because it is a "tangible symbol of the physician's role as a healer" (p. 66). Some people relate the placebo to a hypnotic effect, but Evans asserts that clinical studies do not show this. However, Frank relates it to the trust relationship, the expectancy and even the faith of the patient in the physician. In the same context, Frank says that "until the last few decades most medications prescribed by physicians were pharmacologically inert. That is, physicians were prescribing placebos without knowing it." (These were, one hopes, "honest" placebos, involving little or no deception of the patient.) Since 1962, according to the Louisville *Courier-Journal*, "Federal regulators are about to complete 22 years of testing that has led to the withdrawal of more than 1000 prescription drugs judged to be ineffective" (p. A-3).

Quite apart from the ineffectiveness of medications except for their placebo value, more recent research indicates some biochemical impact of the patient's belief in the placebo. This research into the body's natural pain deterrents, technically identified as **endorphins**, suggests that the placebo may indeed activate the endorphins. A biochemical link to describe *how* the placebo works to relieve pain is now being sought. Glenn Craig Davis says (p. 478):

> Placebo analgesic response may be considered as the recruitment by environmental influences (such as reassurance) of brain pain-suppressing mechanisms. Most types of placebo responses are a function of object-related behavior. That is, an authority, a loved one, a trusted

person suggests or offers an intervention that will reduce pain. This may represent well-developed trusting object-related learned mechanisms. A child who injures himself cries out; this behavior attracts a parent to assess injury. The purpose of the pain and crying out behavior is not only to signal to the child a danger and to aid in learning, but also to attract an adult in a position to do something about the injury or danger. The reassurance offered by the adult may recruit pain-reducing endorphinergenic mechanisms.

It is conceivable, then, that the child's—or the adult's—*belief* in the person providing reassurance has something to do with the body's biological responses.

The ethical concerns about the intentional, premeditated use of placebos has been addressed by Bok, who recommends that placebos be used only after "(1) careful diagnostic workup when no other agents are known to be effective, [when] (2) no other active drugs are being used, (3) no lying to the patient has been done, (4) the patient has not requested that they not be used" (p. 22). Thomas Silber recognizes the "symbolic communication reminiscent of the religious communion . . . to say something words cannot say, that exists between physician and patient." Then he concludes (p. 246):

> Last, but not least, when placebo therapy is given, it needs to be part of a careful clinical plan moving actively in the direction of health. Thus, placebo therapy is accepted as moral when it enhances physician-patient communication and it is accompanied by active efforts to achieve health. Conversely, placebo therapy is viewed as immoral if it diminishes or replaces patient-physician communication and there is no genuine pursuit of health.

The main concern we have here, having dealt with the obvious ethical issues of placebos, is that the patient's perception of pain is a vital component of the whole pain experience. In studies of the placebo response, the ethical factor is not present when the experimenters *themselves* are unaware of who is receiving a placebo and who is not. The very perception of pain itself, both the nerve irritation and the location, size, and quality of pain, is being studied. However, experimental pain does not usually carry with it meanings of illness and threat to self-esteem, freedom from disability, and life itself. Hence, the placebo effect touches only the hem of the garment of the meaning of pain.

Pain Thresholds and Pain Tolerance

Understanding the perception of pain requires careful distinction between pain thresholds and pain tolerance. The **pain threshold** refers to a person's awareness of sensory stimulation of pain. "There is now evidence that all people, regardless of cultural background, have a uniform *sensation threshold*—that is, the lowest stimulus value at which sensation is first reported" (Melzack, 1974b, pp. 24–25). However, the *level of pain tolerance* is that level beyond which the person does not feel he or she can stand any more pain. Individual and cultural backgrounds, age, sex, and so on markedly affect the person's perception of how much pain he or she can tolerate. The recorded experience of Indians, both Native Americans and Far Eastern fakirs, in tolerating pain show that discipline of habits, attention, beliefs, and spiritual commitments shape and even at times determine what effects pain will have on a person's life and integrity.

Attention and the Perception of Pain

Hippocrates (460–351? B.C.) said, "Of two pains occurring together, not in the same part of the body, the stronger weakens the other" (*Aphorisms*, II, 46). This statement seems to imply that the "louder" or "stronger" pain gets the attention. But any kind of pain is heeded by the hurting person. As Ronald Melzack says, "Pain . . . is not only a sensory experience but also has obvious motivational and affective qualities that demand attention" (1974a, p. 275). For example, pain motivates people to move bodily; they have trouble staying still. Pain is frightening, making a person want to fight, flee, or "play dead" by staying as still as possible.

Physicians and psychologists train pain patients to put themselves into a meditational state, thereby distracting attention from the pain site in the body. Persons who pray have done similar things; for example, in Psalm 116:3–4, the psalmist says that "the pangs of [hell] laid hold on me; I suffered distress and anguish. Then I called on the name of the LORD: 'O LORD, I beseech thee, save my life!' " The focus of attention was shifted from the pain to the person of God for help. More will be said later about the discipline of attention in the control of pain. Suffice it to say here that, particularly at the level of pain tolerance, it is within the proximate, but not absolute, power of the patient to do something about his or her capacity to cope with pain.

Pain and Fear/Anxiety

The perception of pain, unless the pain is one to which a person is long accustomed and knows with certainty how to manage, leads to panic. Fear and anxiety mingle with rational thinking. These increase the heart rate, shallow the respiration, and cause the palms to sweat more. Biblical wisdom relates anxiety to shortening of the breath. The body is being prepared to fight or flee from the threat. If pain's threat to the safety, well-being, and comfort of the person were an *external* threat, these responses would be quite useful for survival responses, such as running away from or fighting the threat. However, *internal* pain is intensely increased by such shortening of breath and tightening of muscles. In the next chapter, we will discuss the importance of deep breathing exercises, progressive relaxation, and muscle strengthening and relaxing in the control of pain.

Inner visualizations accompany the anxiety and fear responses to pain. Jean Piaget (p. 356) says that perception has two dimensions, the *operative*, which refers to the internal processes of the organism and resulting actions of thought, such as physiological causes of pain and behavioral responses to pain; and the *figurative*, which involves the mental images and meanings with which the person conceptualizes the pain. For example, a pain may prompt the image of a vise clamping a particular part of the body; the pain patient will tell you, "It is as if a vise were clamping my knee tighter and tighter." A gallbladder pain may be described "as if a knife had been stabbed into my right shoulder blade." This is important to remember in conversation with pain patients. As we come to methods of controlling pain, one of them will be a combination of flooding the area of the pain with attention and changing the imagery to figures of speech that are less threatening and more relaxing than vises and knives.

Paul Tillich's analysis of anxiety is particularly helpful in appreciating the effects of anxiety in a pain patient's life and thought. Tillich describes three types of anxiety: the anxiety of death, the anxiety of meaninglessness, and the anxiety of condemnation and guilt.

The *anxiety of death* in the experience of pain is illustrated in the case of Ivan Ilyich in Tolstoy's novel *The Death of Ivan Ilyich.* The pain he felt was not whether it was coming from this or that kidney but whether he would live or die. Would the malady kill him? Some pain may be associated with lethal disorders, such as cancer or cardiac pain. Other pain only depresses and gives the person death wishes or fears. Paradoxically enough, some pain has a protective element in it that inhibits the person from taking risks that actually kill or at least shorten the life of other people.

The second kind of anxiety Tillich mentions is the *anxiety of meaninglessness.* Does the pain destroy usefulness, disable, and impair the person? Much of the meaning of life comes from work, and a large number of chronic pain patients are on disability. Does the pain itself *become* the central meaning of the person's life? Or, if the person continues to work, does the pain take the joy, zest, and creativity out of the work and produce so much fatigue that little or no energy is left for play? How does the pain syndrome prejudice major decisions and skew the meanings of relationships with family, co-workers, and friends? These are areas for pastoral dialogue with pain patients.

The third anxiety Tillich names is *the anxiety of guilt and condemnation.* Our previous discussion of pain as being historically, linguistically, and spiritually associated in people's perceptions with punishment is a propos here. In many instances, the pain that people experience *is* their own fault—the result of bad judgment, wrong actions, and persistent abuse of their bodies. The traumatic pain of a person who was driving while drunk and had an auto accident, the self-inflicted gunshot wound that left a person maimed and hurting but not dead, the pain of the emphysema patient whose smoking over a lifetime has produced this condition—these people are suffering consequences and may need confession, plans for restitution, and forgiveness.

Tillich says that "all three forms of anxiety are existential in that it belongs to existence as such and not to an abnormal state of mind as in neurotic (and psychotic) anxiety" (1952, pp. 40–41). Having the courage "to be" in the face of the threat of death, of the loss of a spiritual center of ultimate concern, and of moral unacceptability to one's own self—having courage in spite of these is the psychological stuff of which faith is made. To have faith in God is to affirm God's power over death, his capacity to overcome meaninglessness, and his ability to forgive self-condemnation. It is to accept being accepted by God though we are unacceptable to ourselves.

Pain is a threat to ourselves that embodies all three kinds of anxiety Tillich describes. As such, pain is both capable of overwhelming the person with anxiety or provoking the person through anxiety to think through and to discover the deepest sources of his or her relationship to God. A pastor's attentiveness to people in pain is thus a royal road to their spiritual consciousness.

Depression and the Perception of Pain

Richard Sternbach has observed (p. 248) that "in clinical situations, anxiety is associated with the *anticipation* of pain (body harm) or loss (separation). Depression is associated with the *consequence* of these, in the form of intropunitive anger, or of mourning." More than being angry at oneself and mourning because of loss, depression is also a profound feeling of helplessness and loss of control. In both acute and chronic pain states, but especially chronic states, a sleep disorder, a pronounced irritability, a saddening of mood, a loss of enjoyment in life follows as night does day. These take on pathological proportions and lead to clinical depression, even to suicidal thoughts and preparations. The depression exists alongside the pain disorder. The pain patient's coping measures become exhausted. He or she is trapped in a seemingly "no exit" situation.

Such a patient's perception of the world is distorted by the depression. As we say, he or she sees the world through the darkest of glasses. Perception of other persons is skewed. Poor judgment results. Indecision and faulty decisions follow the poor judgment. D. C. Turk and R. D. Kerns quote a patient suffering from migraine headaches (p. 60).

> For hours and hours, God will it [pain] ever end? How much longer do I have to live this way? I have outlived my capacities . . . the hours are endless and I am alone. I wish someone would take a sharp scalpel and cut that artery. . . . How long will it be until I am sent to a mental institution? Migraines are not fatal, doctors do not care. You live through one only to be struck with another in a few days. I am incapable of everything I used to do. How am I going to fill the rest of my life? . . . Unemployed, capable of so little, and increasingly alone.

In one study of 100 chronic pain patients (Kramlinger et al.), 25 percent were definitely depressed and 39 percent were probably depressed. The combined treatment of the pain disorder and the depression in the 25 percent who were definitely depressed resulted in an 88 percent recovery from the depression.

The working connection between the chronic pain and the depression is the sleep disorder, plus the hopelessness and helplessness of the patient. In a wide range of pain syndromes—cancer pain, arthritis, atypical facial pain, headaches, different neuralgias, and back pain—physicians have found the antidepressant medications such as amitriptyline (Elavil), imipramine (Tofranil), doxepin (Sinequan), and others to be doubly useful, according to T. Declan Walsh. These alleviate both the pain and the depression. More than this, they enable the patient to think more constructively and to talk more rationally about his or her life and destiny as a person. The hazard of addiction to these medications is very low. However, if the patient is suicidal, only small quantities of these antidepressants should be within reach. They could be used lethally in suicide attempts. Likewise, the exact dosage prescribed should be followed scrupulously.

The pastor's opportunity in the care of the depressed pain patient is increased if the patient has a physician who treats both the pain and the depression. For the devoutly religious person who may resist the use of any drugs, the pastor can support the *disciplined* use of antidepressants and other medication. As Paul said, "Everything created by God is good, and nothing is to be rejected if it is received with thanksgiving; for then it is consecrated by the word of God and prayer" (1 Tim. 4:4–5). For the Christian, the cautious, disciplined, and physician-monitored use of medications *can* be a form of prayer.

The Communication of the Meaning of Pain

"Pain," says H. K. Beecher, "cannot be satisfactorily defined, except as each man defines it for himself" (1957, p. 190). The patient's definition is a private one with swift successions of images appearing in his or her personal perception. Even so, the patient seeks to tell other people about the hurt. This communication begins at the nonverbal level.

Nonverbal Signs of Pain

Nonverbal signs of pain are elaborate and dramatic. Some of them are:

Changes in breathing. When pain hits a person, he or she catches the breath suddenly, momentarily stops breathing, and sighs when the pain abates. Anxiety that the pain will strike again will shorten the breath, and the patient begins to pant. When the pain releases for any length of time, breathing returns to an easy rhythm.

Utterances too deep for words. Groans, cries, wails, and screams of pain are forms of communication, but they are utterances too deep for words. They are a strange but universal kind of glossolalia. Such utterances of pain are similar to a small infant's rudimentary language. As Tennyson asked in *In Memoriam,* so does the pain patient often feel:

> But what am I?
> An infant crying in the night;

An infant crying for the light;
And with no language but a cry.

The patient who leaves his or her efforts to be interpreted by others at this level of meaning has great difficulty in being understood and even more in being accepted by medical and nursing personnel or taken seriously by family members. A pastor, skilled in the use of words to express feelings, can "tutor" the patient in choosing words that locate, describe, and interpret the course of the pain experience. The pastor is uniquely equipped to search for sense in the syllables of cries, groans, screams, and sighs.

The choreography of pain. Not only do wordless sounds communicate pain, movements of the body do also. Jumping, jerking, cringing, grimacing, squirming, limping, and flinching are just a few of the graphic movements that pain elicits in a person. Facial tenseness, clenched hands, hands drawn to the head, the neck, the back all tend to say, "I hurt right here." In structured interviews of pain patients by Paul Cinciripini and Alice Floreen, gestures and touching of others ranked higher in frequency than laughter, eye contact, and several other forms of nonverbal actions. The pastor learns to "listen with the eyes" when conversing with persons in pain. Aristotle said that life is movement or motion. The patient in pain tells you much about his or her inner life in bodily movements. A remarkably well-researched book, *Bodily Movements in Psychotherapy* by David Steere, a distinguished pastoral counselor, thoroughly discusses the communicative power of movements. He makes much of how childlike states of awareness, expressed most vividly in our bodily movements, are often more honest and accurate than our words. The choreography of pain indeed reveals the pain-ridden person as having both the language of the cry, as Tennyson put it, and the language of movement, as Aristotle put it.

The pastoral task, then, is to change nonverbal language behavior to the kinds of behaviors that are chosen voluntarily, not just done impulsively at first and then repeated as meaningless, fatiguing, and isolating habits. The whole discipline of physiotherapy concerns teaching and learning behaviors that genuinely relieve pain, rather than doing nothing or actually contributing to it, by isolating the person from family, friends, church, and the larger community. As Sigmund Freud pointed out in 1914 (p. 82):

It is universally known, and we take it as a matter of course, that a person who is tormented by organic pain and discomfort gives up his interest in the things of the external world, in so far as they do not concern his suffering. Closer observation teaches us that he also withdraws *libidinal* interest from his love-objects: so long as he suffers, he ceases to love.

7

A Way of Life
for Controlling Pain

Acute pain is a time-limited experience. A kidney stone produces excruciating pain, but not forever. When the stone passes naturally or is removed surgically, the pain subsides. More positively, a mother in labor suffers pain that she knows will be over after delivery. As Jesus said, "When a woman is in travail she has sorrow, because her hour has come; but when she is delivered of the child, she no longer remembers the anguish, for joy that a child is born into the world" (John 16:21). Even cancer pain prompts the patient to think of death as a deliverance, an end to the hurting.

However, other kinds of pain are endless. Arthritic patients, persons with migraine headaches, severe facial and neck pain, or low back pain, and sufferers of many other kinds of chronic pain neither see nor feel that their pain will ever be over. Physicians are likely to say to such patients, "This is something you will have to learn to live with." Some people hear this as a sort of doom and give in to their pain all the more. Other patients are wise enough to ask the physician to provide instructions for learning how to live with their pain. Their curiosity is turned on by the challenge of learning a way of life that lessens, helps to manage, and enables them to control their pain states. Hope is generated that will put them to learning ways of preventing their pain from causing them to deteriorate as persons.

You as a pastor can be a part of enabling patients to learn concrete patterns of living that will go a long way toward helping them continue to be productive persons, rather than deteriorating as human beings under the impact of persistent pain. Such people may learn things about life itself that otherwise they would have ignored, missed, or thought inapplicable. These very learnings may even enlarge, enrich, and ennoble their lives. What are some of these learnings?

The Vicious Cycle of Pain

Tissue damage from abrasion, trauma, inflammation, or a growth sets in motion a vicious cycle. The first reaction is shock and alarm, which causes the person to brace or flinch against the impulses of pain. This is accompanied by gasping and shortening of the breath. These are the physiological components of anxiety. The end result is a tightening of muscles that eventually go into spasm and increase the pain all the more. The cycle is repeated. This is the vicious cycle of pain at the physiological and psychological levels.

The cycle expands to the broader functions of the person's life. Escalating pain such as has just been described sets in motion a quintet of personal and social reactions.

Sleep Disorder

Chronic pain will keep the patient from finding a comfortable position for going to sleep. Having finally dropped off, the person may be jolted upright as relaxing muscles backfire into involuntary spasms. If he or she goes back to sleep, staying in one position for any length of time may increase the pain, and this often awakens the patient again. Struggling to return to sleep without success may increase the pain. After finally getting back to sleep, the person may sleep until the normal rising time, only to face the day unrested. Night after night of this kind of stress-ridden sleep accumulates the tiredness.

Exhaustion

Pain uses energy. The loss of sleep drains energy further. Deprivation of energy impairs the ability to respond accurately or forcefully to anything. Exhaustion is part of the process of stress which Hans Selye calls "the general adaptation syndrome." If we think of pain as the stressor that it is, then a person, according to Selye, reacts first with *alarm*—"a call to arms of the defensive forces in the organism." Then, in the second phase, the whole being of a person reorganizes in *resistance.* For example, in the alarm phase the stores of the adrenal gland are decreased. In the resistance phase the gland accumulates a reserve supply. After prolonged exposure to noxious agents, "this acquired adaptation is lost." This is the third phase, *exhaustion*. The "wear and tear" factor of stress as Selye describes it (pp. 36–37) is a part of the vicious cycle of pain. At this point the pain patient tends to panic. The stress moves outward from the private world to interpersonal spheres.

Interpersonal Conflict, Cooperation, and Pain Games

The vicious cycle of pain moves from the private world of the patient to those in the social support system of fellow humans, the family of orientation (father, mother, brothers, and sisters) and the family of procreation (spouse and children). If the person is employed outside the home, associates are affected by the pain patient's decreased ability to work, by absenteeism, and by the impending possibility of disability retirement. Even if the person is not employed outside the home, household duties tend to be shifted to other members of the family. Roles are often reversed and overloaded, with the pain-free spouse doing both breadwinning and home duties and the pain patient being inactive and immobilized. Subtle shifts in lines of authority, attention-receiving, and expectations occur.

The most notable thing about these shifts in the family relationships of people in pain is that they occur slowly; patient and family will drift into stress-producing rather than stress-relieving patterns of relating to each other. You as a pastor may perceive the family as a system of systems delicately affecting one another; then the experience of pain in one member becomes a radiating force affecting the whole family. Next, these effects penetrate the family's relationship to the church of which they are members. Probably the most visible and audible relationship you see and hear discussed is how the pain patient thinks, feels, and acts toward doctors and medications.

In these interpersonal relationships, helplessness, manipulative games, and rage become apparent. We simply point to these effects here; they are a part of the vicious cycle of pain. A more detailed discussion appears in the next section.

Interrupting and Reversing the Vicious Cycle of Pain

The cycle of pain can be interrupted. It can be reversed. In many instances, it can be the catalyst for the patient's learning a whole new way of life, of becoming transformed into a new kind of human being. How does this happen?

Removing the Mystery and the Fictions of Pain

Adequate, thorough, and patient diagnosis of the pain state, cou-
pled with thorough teaching of the patient, is the first step in breaking the vicious cycle of pain. This removes the images in the patient's mind that amount to a belief system about what is wrong. The
pain-ridden person develops a personal theory, or "fiction," as to
what causes the pain. For example, unexplainable pain easily trig-
gers fear of cancer. A person who has had previous pain (relieved
by surgery) that occurs in the same location may imagine that the
old condition has returned. This is not to suggest that the patient
is suffering from imaginary pain or pain of purely psychological
origin. To the contrary, the assumption is that the pain is real, and
has a verifiable cause, but that the patient has simply formed a
self-diagnosis that is not founded on fact. It is another version of the
saying that "the person who has himself or herself for a doctor has
a fool for a patient." An objective diagnosis by a physician is
needed.

If pain persists over a period of time, the person with the pain is
likely to complain to those nearby. These persons in turn will make
similar homemade diagnoses, such things as "It is probably something you ate" or "You've been working too hard and need some
rest" or "You worry too much and are just tense" or "You've been
under a lot of pressure." However, if the pain persists, they are
likely to urge the person to see a doctor. In other words, before a
doctor is considered, both patient and "significant others," as these
associates are called, form their own versions of what is wrong.
Once their hypotheses begin to lose credibility, they are faced with
the mystery of the pain and begin to think of seeking medical assistance. Religious persons may resort to spiritual admonitions in keeping with a particular set of beliefs and attitudes as discussed in
chapter 1. However, once family and friends are convinced of the
pain's mystery, they usually begin urging the patient to consult a
physician.

As a pastor you are often consulted by persons in pain about any
of a large variety of personal problems. They may or may not think
to share with you that they are also in physical pain, so a routine part
of your interview should be to inquire into the health and well-being
of these persons. How is the wear and tear of life affecting their
physical health? Are they experiencing any pain in their body? Just
because an occasional parishioner puts "aches and pains" at the top
of the list should not deter you from routinely asking all people who
consult you about the amount and kind of pain they are carrying

with them at the time. On the basis of the data already given in this book, you can become a part of each pain-ridden person's effort to remove the fiction and mystery of pain, suggest the assistance of a capable physician, and help break the vicious cycle of pain as soon as possible.

The reflective pastor can be of assistance to the person who does not have a physician. Referral to a specialist in internal medicine is a good first step in the diagnosis of pain states. The internist is by definition a diagnostician and is trained to make referrals to other specialists—such as orthopedists, neurologists, rheumatologists, physiatrists (specialists in physical medicine and rehabilitation), neurosurgeons, and psychiatrists—who focus their expertise on different pain states. Orthopedic surgeons and neurosurgeons are usually the persons who perform surgery, although general surgeons will operate on cancer patients and a wide range of other persons suffering from such painful conditions as stomach ulcers or gallstones.

Pastoral intervention by way of referral seems best done by your sending the person to an internist, a neurologist, or a physiatrist, or to a combination of these, *before* they go to a surgeon. Thus the patient has the advantage of two opinions before the radical measure of surgery is chosen. This does not say anything about surgeons except that surgery for chronic pain is always a last solution rather than a first one. Even then, more than one medical opinion is needed as to the wisdom of surgery, over against more conservative measures for the relief of pain. Then, too, the pain patient may be so eager to be "cured" that he or she will impose magical expectations upon the surgeon for complete relief, when the result may in fact be only partial relief or no relief at all.

Pain Games

The preceding discussion introduces the factor of gamesmanship, which confuses both the pain patient and those who are called upon to treat the pain and to care for the patient, whether they be physicians or the patient's family. These interpersonal maneuvers are found in pain disorders that are of psychogenic origin and even in pain disorders that have severe lesions, trauma, or inflammations as the source of the pain. In a sense, "pain games," as they are named by Richard Sternbach and others, are shorthand ways of identifying how pain is used as a form of communication. George Engel calls these ways of relating to other people the pain patient's "psychic signature." Thomas Szasz uses the term "painsmanship" rather than "gamesmanship," which is a concept broadly applied by Eric Berne to many kinds of human relationships.

Sternbach (p. 424) describes a patient-doctor game as follows:

> The patient says to the doctor: "I hurt. Please fix me." (But you can't.)
> The doctor says to the patient: "I'll fix you."
> After many different procedures are tried and all of them fail, the patient says to the doctor (in righteous indignation): "Another incompetent quack!"
> Then the doctor says defensively: "Another contrary noncompliant crock!"
> Each tends to write the other off in exasperation. One of the results of this interchange is that the patient goes from doctor to doctor repeating the same scenario until a physician anticipates it and is able to promise little and react with openness on the first interview.

In the family setting, pain becomes the conductor of all communication between the patient and his or her family. Love, hostility, sexuality, work, play, and even worship are transacted through the medium of the patient's pain. It becomes the controlling motif. In fact, it is a reciprocal game in that family members come to express affection, attention, and all other concerns in terms of the patient's pain. He or she, in turn, tends to control other members of the family through the pain.

One of the ways family therapists have dealt with this kind of interaction is to see the whole family as a unit in the same interview. As a pastor you can do this also, either on home visits or in office interviews. The first two or three meetings can be used in getting an empathic understanding of the struggles of family members in dealing with the suffering. Then you can make a covenant with them to use the first ten minutes of each subsequent interview to deal with anything new that the pain patient has experienced in pain. After the first ten minutes, the covenant will be to discuss other concerns that the family as a whole has. Thus the pain is taken seriously and updated, but it is not allowed to be the main and only focus of concern. This effectively calls off the game for the whole family. The pain patient is no longer either the culprit or the victim but is now as concerned with other members' problems as with personal ones.

In the workplace, gamesmanship occurs in the multiple issues of whether or not the person will go on disability, whether or not he or she will pick and choose duties in terms of the pain states, whether or not he or she will expect to be "covered" by close friends on the job, and so on. This particular concern will be discussed more fully in chapter 8 on the pain patient's sense of vocation.

A bizarre example of painsmanship is the condition known as Munchausen's syndrome, named after Baron von Munchausen (1720–1797). This is a severe personality disorder wherein a person malingers or consciously feigns an illness to obtain a desired end. Some people do this repeatedly. They go from hospital to hospital, often under assumed names, always telling the same story and submitting to innumerable medical investigations and operations. Baron von Munchausen entertained his friends with extraordinary and untrue tales of his supposed adventures and gained the reputation of being an incorrigible liar. This bizarre behavior displays the meaning of painsmanship in large print so that only the blind can fail to see. Smaller print versions occur subtly in the lives of many chronic pain patients, who nevertheless have bona fide pain syndromes.

Positive Life Changes for the Pain Patient

As you can see, much negative behavior and many thought patterns must be dealt with to clear the way for positive changes that will do more than just break the vicious cycle of pain. Specific positive ways of thinking and behaving are available almost as the counterparts of some of the aspects of the vicious cycle of pain.

Focusing vs. Diverting Attention

In chapter 6, attention was considered as one of the psychological factors in setting the stage for the perception of pain. Perception must be differentiated from attention. We attend to something in order to perceive it. However, paying attention is focusing on a limited range of stimuli and becoming aware of them. Perception is the process of interpreting what those stimuli mean. Therefore, pain patients have some control over what they are going to attend to and how they are going to interpret that to which they attend. For this degree of personal control, the patient is responsible. The beginning of a positive approach to pain control occurs when the physician, the physiotherapist, the family, and you as pastor inspire the patient to believe that he or she is not helpless but has this power of control over attention.

The commonsense approach to the process of attention is to divert the patient from constantly thinking about pain. In a way, to ration the patient to ten minutes of an interview in which new data about the pain are discussed is to divert attention to something else. Also, many pain patients will say that the pain they suffer is worse when they are off from work, with leisure time to think about it. Consequently, they keep busy and often exhaust themselves to distract their attention from their pain state. Yet when they finally let down and relax, they begin to suffer more pain, not just because they have time to think about it but also because they are fatigued beyond the point of resting very well at all. For such a person, stopping work and going on a vacation would best be done by a stepdown of activity by stages rather than all at once. Diverted attention combined with feverish devotion to work is destructive and can become idolatrous. The other side of the dilemma, however, is that a clear sense of mission in one's work keeps pain from becoming an all-consuming vocation in its own right.

Constructive methods of focusing attention on pain are rewarding many patients with measures of relief and even some cure of the source of the pain itself. The most used of these methods is relaxation through inner visualization and deep breathing. As pastor, you can develop a personal *and* pastoral program of systematic relaxation, first for yourself and then in relation to persons undergoing severe anxiety and tension-provoking events, of which pain is one. Background reading for this should include Edmund Jacobson's *Anxiety and Tension Control: A Physiologic Approach,* Herbert Benson and Miriam Klipper's *The Relaxation Response,* and Carl Simonton's *Getting Well Again: A Step-by-Step Self-Help Guide to Overcoming Cancer for Patients and Their Families.* The inner visualization and deep-breathing approach to focusing attention systematically upon the locus of the pain has been reported by Simonton to be especially helpful with persons suffering from cancer pain. The person with any kind of chronic pain can profit from its use.

The patient sits in a comfortable chair with feet resting at ease on the floor, hands and arms loosely resting on the arms of the chair, and eyes closed. The patient is told to breathe deeply, all the while visualizing the path of the air from the nostrils to the throat to the lungs to the diaphragm, and then exhale, retracing in the imagination the course of the expelled air. After eight or ten deep breaths, the person is told to focus on the specific location of the pain and visualize exactly what shape and size the hurting spot or spots may be in the "mind's eye."

Then the patient is urged to use the imagination to compress the pain into a smaller area. A pen and paper are offered, to draw a picture of what the pain area is like. After this, the patient is asked to talk with the therapist about what he or she has visualized. Then the patient is encouraged to concentrate on this visual image and think of a favorite color that is warm and soothing as saturating the pain area. Then the deep-breathing and inner-visualization exercises are repeated.

This highly intentional focusing of attention on the pain itself, when repeated two or three times daily, will paradoxically reduce the amount of pain the patient suffers. Some researchers insist that it tends to remove the noxious cause of the pain. To say the least, it has a way of turning the locale of the pain into a friendly area rather than enemy territory. It is a specific relaxation procedure for untightening the musculature of the area and easing the muscles from a combative posture to a more peaceful one. As Norman Cousins says in his book *The Anatomy of an Illness*, pain is not the ultimate enemy. Inner-visualization and deep-breathing exercises have the unique result of getting the patient on friendlier terms with his or her pain and out of armed combat. At the least the pain becomes a "friendly enemy."

Dealing with Depression and Sleeplessness

We have seen that depression and sleeplessness, which are inseparable, are both caused by and contribute to a chronic pain disorder. An escalating spiral of hopelessness, helplessness, and increasingly poor judgment complicates a pain disorder of any extended duration.

Your supportive presence as a pastor cuts down on the pain patient's isolation. Depressed pain patients feel cut off from other people. They think that no one understands how they feel and that words are not available to help them understand. They give up trying. You provide companionship in the suffering. In addition, you remind the person both nonverbally and verbally of the presence of God in daytime struggles with pain and in the long night watches of sleeplessness. At the same time, you keep a watchful eye out for the basic signs of depression. What are they?

Diagnostic signs of depression are:

Poor appetite and weight loss, or increased appetite and significant weight gain

Sleeplessness

Mental and physical agitation or immobility

Loss of interest and pleasure in life, particularly a decrease in sexual interest and ability

Feelings of worthlessness, self-reproach, or excessive or inappropriate guilt feelings

Complaints or evidence of inability to think, remember, or
make decisions

Recurrent thoughts of death, wishes to be dead, suicidal idea-
tion, or suicidal attempts

You as a pastor wisely take into consideration whether or not the
particular pain patient has any organic mental disorder such as
would be true of a person who, in addition to being in pain, had
suffered a severe head injury or was suffering from dementia of one
kind or another. These are often attended by depression. Also, you
weigh the above characteristics of depression differently if the person has suffered a severe bereavement recently. Bereavement is a
normal depression.

Your pastoral consultation with and referral to the physician of
a patient who shows the above signs of depression is of utmost
importance. K. G. Kramlinger and other physicians at the Mayo
Clinic studied 100 consecutive patients suffering from chronic pain:
25 were definitely depressed, 39 were probably depressed, and only
36 were not depressed. Remarkably, 88 of these patients were suffering pain in the back, arms, and legs, or all three; 6 of them
suffered "total pain" all over. On discharge from the pain clinic, 88
percent were free of depression.

There seems to be a circular relation of pain and depression:
transient pain complaints are made by depressed patients, and depression accompanies chronic pain states. "Many chronic pain syndromes are thought to be intimately affected by the patients' personality as well as their mood. Many antidepressant [medications]
have both a sedative and an analgesic action, and it has been suggested that much of their therapeutic action is due to their sedative
effect." It is also hypothesized that antidepressant medications increase the action of the body's own pain-killing agents. We do know
that the pain reduction is aided by increasing serotinin in the central
nervous system at both the limbic and spinal-cord levels (Walsh, pp.
277–278). The clinically demonstrated fact is that antidepressant
medications do help to correct the sleep disorder of chronic pain
patients within 48 hours, and the sleep itself seems to produce
positive relief from pain. Over a period of 10 to 14 days, antidepressants help to lift the depression the person suffers as well.

One of the most helpful aspects of these medications is that they
free the patient from the necessity of sedatives that in themselves

will add to depression, and that at the same time can become addictive. Also, they help to avoid the use of opiate painkillers, which can become addictive also.

Consequently, you can be of great service to pain patients by urging them to discuss their medications, their depression, and their sleeplessness with their physician. We can expect that, in turn, the physician will use these more recent approaches to the multiple problems the patients present. You yourself can serve as a conversationalist and counselor with the person about the effects that the depression and its attendant hopelessness have on his or her spiritual outlook on life. Such people should be seen often for brief interviews, rather than infrequently for long interviews. One important result of the antidepressant medications is that in many instances they enable the person to think, talk, and act more rationally and with less of a sense of panic about the management of their lives and their responsibilities to other people and to God.

More extensive discussions of the pastoral care of depressed persons can be found in Roy Fairchild's book *Finding Hope Again: A Pastor's Guide to Counseling Depressed Persons* and Janice Wood Wetzel's *The Clinical Handbook of Depression.*

Being a part of bringing hope to persons is one of your primary functions as a pastor. The hopelessness and helplessness of people in pain is a primary focus of attention in your pastoral care. You can always look for these conditions and respond meaningfully to them in your ministry to persons in chronic pain. Being sensitive to what George Engel called the "giving up and giving in complex" of emotions is a positive commitment for any pastor involved in the care of the pain patient, and for anyone else, for that matter.

The Exercise–Rest Balance

A discussion of depression invariably involves the patient's need for rest and sleep. However, this need must be kept in balance with the complementary need for appropriate and healing exercise. Lack of movement contributes to pain as certainly as does a lack of rest and sleep. Muscular tissue can atrophy from lack of use. Pain itself discourages a person from movement and exercise.

Here again, as pastor, you should consider whether a specific exercise will contribute to or militate against the patient's control of pain. The whole task of physiotherapists is concerned with the wise restoration of the patient's use of the body. Whether a person is an accident victim, a stroke patient, or a burn patient, or is suffering from chronic pain, the physiotherapist carries out a physician's prescription of bodily movements in order to teach the patients to use their bodies to best advantage in independent living to the greatest extent possible. Increasing physical activity decreases depression and feelings of helplessness. Physiotherapy is a social experience that shifts attention from pain to what can be done about it.

Therefore, as a pastor or chaplain you would do well to collaborate with physiotherapists in understanding their overall work and the specific work they are doing with a given patient. The pain patient's own report of what he or she has learned from the physiotherapist will be intriguing to you, because you are eager to learn directly from the patient. If you visit while a patient is in the physical therapy area of a hospital, simply watching and helping to celebrate each new achievement can be a form of spiritual grace for both patient and therapist. Especially is this so if you do not interfere with the process physically by getting in the way of what has to be done.

Arthritic patients and back pain patients, who make up a large percentage of all chronic pain patients, are often given exercises that are to be practiced ritually every day. Walking, swimming, or stationary biking may be encouraged. These are health measures for persons without pain disorders, too; you can set an example and model these programs for pain patients. The comradery that develops is another form of koinonia. You are at work always creating a sense of community, of belonging, of fellowship. Exercise groups are becoming more and more a part of the activity programs of churches. You can encourage these groups and insist on qualified and wise leadership for them.

Positive Reworking of Food, Alcohol, and Drug Use

The anxiety and depression that accompany chronic pain conspire to push a pain patient toward pain assuagement, which in this context means to pacify but not to give reliable or lasting relief. At least three different substances create the illusion of well-being—food, alcohol, and drugs of one kind or another—but the illusion simply calls for more of the substance rather than providing genuine control of anxiety, depression, or pain. You should listen carefully for references the pain patient may make to the use of one or more of these substances. Similarly, you can observe their effects on the appearance and behavior of the patient. As the degree of trust, respect, and rapport between yourself and the patient increases with time and contact, you can ask questions directly.

Eating is not only a means to good nutrition, it is also a solace to a person plagued with pain. If the person is also disabled to the point where time hangs heavy, food is a way of handling boredom. Imperceptibly, however, it adds weight, especially when aided and abetted by inactivity. Overweight can and does add to pain, especially in cases of chronic low back pain and osteoarthritis in other parts of the body, such as the thighs, knees, legs, and feet. Overweight becomes a severe complicating factor in the amount and intensity of pain.

The most common way of dealing with overweight is to go on a diet and attempt to lose large amounts of weight in a short time. These diets do not often bring results, and when they do, they are not lasting. The person soon reverts to old ways of eating, the weight returns, and the person becomes discouraged and has a low self-estimate because of this "lack of willpower." Therefore, your pastoral instruction is best when dieting is avoided. Your plain injunction "Don't go on a diet" will catch the person's attention.

The constructive alternative is to determine what the person's normal calorie need is, based on height, weight, and level of exercise—sedentary, moderate, or active—on a lifelong basis.

A woman's base weight is said to be 100 pounds for 5 feet of height. For each inch *over* 5 feet, add 5 pounds to the base weight of 100 pounds; subtract five pounds for each inch *under* 5 feet.

For men, the base weight would be 106 pounds for 5 feet of height. For each inch *over* 5 feet, add 6 pounds to the base weight; subtract 6 pounds for each inch *under* 5 feet.

The next step is to check the level of activity at which a person functions. This means the amount of physical exercise involved in the person's normal way of life.

If the person is sedentary and does little more than light housework or office work, the activity factor is calculated at a numeral of 12.

If the person is moderately active in general housework, physical labor on a job, fast walking and moving about, the activity factor is 15.

If the person is very active in heavy housecleaning or other heavy work, or is involved in much fast walking or sports, the activity factor is 18.

At this point, if you multiply the person's ideal weight by the activity factor, you will get their approximate daily caloric need. For example, a man 6 feet 1 inch tall has an ideal weight of 184 pounds. If he is moderately active, to multiply his normal weight by an activity factor of 15 reveals his normal calorie intake to be about 2,760 calories per day. One pound of weight equals 3,500 calories.

If a person whose calorie intake is normally 2,760 calories a day carefully cuts 500 calories per day or 3,500 calories over a week's time, he or she will tend to lose about 1 pound a week. If this is kept up over a year's time, 52 pounds can be gradually lost. The reduction of 250 calories per day from a normal food and drink intake would enable a person to lose 26 pounds in a year. Little adjustment of that pattern of eating for the rest of the person's life would be needed to maintain that ideal weight.

This would require a person to learn how most wisely to "spend" calories. Cutting out junk foods, second helpings, in-between meal snacking, and high calorie–low food value foods and drinks will go a long way toward pulling the calorie intake back to a normal level. Turning toward fruits instead of desserts, limiting bread intake, and avoiding high-calorie sauces, dressings, and gravies will pull the intake down to a level where a modest but steady weight loss can occur. Meanwhile the person does not feel that he or she is starving to death, getting headaches, weak feelings, and being preoccupied with thoughts of food at all times. In brief, this is a way of life for sensible eating, not a diet plan.

People adopting such a way of life need all the encouragement and positive reinforcement possible—from family and friends, from their physician, and from you as their pastor. Many times family members will want to *do* something for the pain patient. One such thing is to *feed* the person. This is not rational, but it does happen.

Alcohol is another substance that lures the pain patient into overusing it. The fact that alcohol was used as an anesthetic before the discovery of more powerful and controllable forms of anesthesia points to the ways in which alcohol can dull the sources and perception of pain. Also, because alcohol is readily available without prescription, it is easy for the person in pain to self-medicate in isolation from other people—family, pastor, physician, or anyone else.

Yet alcohol may increase the amount of depression a person in pain is experiencing. At the same time, when used to the point of drunkenness, alcohol reduces whatever level of function—in work, driving a car, relating responsibly to family and friends—that the person may have left after the ravages of pain have done their worst. (For the latest definitive book, get George Vaillant's *The Natural History of Alcoholism.*)

Alcohol, furthermore, is a drug, in company with a large number of other drugs that are often used in conjunction with alcohol. Some of these are prescription drugs, and getting them becomes a part of the gamesmanship of pain patients. One of their most common ploys is to move from one physician to another without letting these physicians know that several doctors are being literally shopped for prescriptions.

As a pastor, you usually have to rely upon observation, family reports, and collaboration with physicians to be informed about the pain patient's abuse of drugs. This is especially true if the patient uses illegal drugs such as marijuana or cocaine, to alleviate pain. Sometimes the patient will feel so guilty about these excesses that in a state of remorse, which is a part of the addictive process, he or she will develop a sudden but frantic interest in religion and confess to using the substances to you.

Do not assume that a patient is likely to be addicted. Fear of addiction keeps many pain patients from taking minimum amounts even of nonaddictive medications. Some patients have a stoical attitude about pain and think they should be able to "take it." Others, such as the cancer patients studied by John Bonica of the University of Washington, are often undermedicated because of the reluctance of physicians to prescribe enough medication for them. Yet some cancer patients learn enough meditative skills that they prefer being conscious of events to being "out of it" with painkillers.

The important pastoral dimension of these behaviors is that the pain patient has become all the more isolated, assuaging not only the pain but also the loneliness that he or she feels. The best antidote for this isolation is for the person to become a part of a community of other people suffering from pain and perhaps also from abuse of such things as Demerol, Darvon, barbiturates, and street drugs. It is entirely feasible for you as a pastor to form a group of such persons and to learn from the wisdom that Alcoholics Anonymous has to offer on the value of such self-help groups. Or you can urge the patient to participate in organizations such as Alcoholics Anonymous, Emotions Anonymous, and Overeaters Anonymous. You and your congregation can go even further by offering such groups the hospitality of your church building for a place to meet.

Your major temptation as a pastor in dealing with a person who is blatantly alcoholic is to focus so much attention on the drinking problem that you will miss the pain. Your assessment is not to provide an excuse for the alcoholism but to ask whether the alcoholism is a very bad attempt at pain control. To shift the topic of conversation from family problems, job problems, and alcohol addiction to the pain problem forms an unexpected basis of your pastoral relationship. Then, too, alcoholism is related to many primary causes of pain, such as automobile accidents, burn accidents, liver damage, and heart disorder. Your taking seriously the pain that arises from these disorders is a form of compassion. A person with an alcohol or other drug-dependent problem then feels understood and appreciated as a fellow human being without at the same time being patronized or dealt with moralistically or sentimentally.

Coming to Terms with Overwork

In chapter 8, full attention will be given to the spiritual dimensions of the work and vocation of the pain patient. Suffice it to say here that many pain patients have a constant disability that clouds their getting free of pain, doing things that will lessen if not eradicate the pain, and doing things that will assure that pain does not become their main concern in life.

On the other hand, there are patients who use work as a means of warding off the thoughts and perceptions of their pain. They have trouble sitting still, lying still, standing still. They are in ceaseless activity. Work becomes a foil with which to cope with pain. This can happen to such an extent that the person does not get the rest that is needed to do what relaxation and sleep alone can do to ward off, lessen, and heal the pain itself. Work addiction can become a counterproductive force in the life of a person coping with chronic pain.

Offsetting Loneliness with an Intimate Community

A common thread running through this discussion of positive approaches to the management of pain is the need of patients to discover an intimate community of persons to which they can belong, from which they can receive spiritual energy, with which they can participate in suffering, and for which they can care. The apostle Paul spoke of this kind of community with God and our neighbor in 2 Corinthians 1:3–7:

> Blessed be the God and Father of our Lord Jesus Christ, the Father of mercies and God of all comfort, who comforts us in all our affliction, so that we may be able to comfort those who are in any affliction, with the comfort with which we ourselves are comforted by God. For as we share abundantly in Christ's sufferings, so through Christ we share abundantly in comfort too. If we are afflicted, it is for your comfort and salvation; and if we are comforted, it is for your comfort, which you experience when you patiently endure the same sufferings that we suffer. Our hope for you is unshaken; for we know that as you share in our sufferings, you will also share in our comfort.

You as a pastor represent this fellowship of suffering of all kinds. You need not feel helpless in ministering to the patient with chronic pain, even if the work carries frustration with it. In your person and in your spiritual realism about the limitations of the human situation, your own steadfast faithfulness to the person in pain, "through thick and thin," is an effective antidote to loneliness. The fellowship of other people in the church can be mobilized into a system of support to bridge the chasms of loneliness that the person in pain feels. Such a fellowship can make the addictions we have talked about less necessary and therefore less powerful.

The disciplines we have discussed—relaxation, mastery of depression, control of weight, control of the abuse of alcohol and other drugs—can be set within a context of spiritual strength from God. Admitting that one is powerless to combat pain and putting one's life into the hands of God are no idle steps to take, as every committed member of Alcoholics Anonymous has discovered. To be "laid hold of" by a God who is both powerful and friendly is to begin to relax tense muscles, cease to add to the pain, and cease to be alone. In Jesus Christ, the facing of possible death becomes less threatening. The conviction of the reality of the resurrection has a way both of transforming the meaning of pain and of lifting a hurting person above its power to debilitate. Even the capacity to laugh at pain is helpful. As Norman Cousins says of his own pain (p. 39), "Nothing is less funny than being flat on your back with all the bones in your spine and joints hurting. . . . I made the joyous discovery that ten minutes of genuine belly laugh had an anesthetic effect and would give me two hours of pain-free sleep." A sense of humor and a lively curiosity are rarely identified as marks of a genuinely Christian way of life. However, seeing ourselves from the perspective of the Eternal and accepting the assurances of Jesus Christ have a way of generating humor and a vivid curiosity. When these are focused on the pain experience, a positive way of life in understanding pain, managing pain, and reducing it to a minimum has begun. You can be a catalyst of the perspective of the Eternal and the assurances of Jesus Christ.

8

Spiritual Concerns
of the Pain Patient

Your function as a pastor in relation to the patient in pain is primarily centered in his or her relationship to God and neighbor. Alfred North Whitehead said that our relationship to God fluctuates between perceiving God as an enemy, as a void, and as a friend. Our very presence as pastors connotes all three perceptions of God to the person in pain. Instead of feeling one way consistently toward God, the patient's affective response to the very thought of God moves back and forth among all three of the perceptions of which Whitehead speaks.

Similarly, the moods Elisabeth Kübler-Ross associates with grief —denial, anger, bargaining, depression, and acceptance—are translatable into religious affections, to use Jonathan Edwards's description of the spiritual life in his *Treatise Concerning the Religious Affections.* Consequently, pain patients look up to you as an interpreter of their distress in prayer before God and as a searcher with them of the mysteries of their relationship to God in spiritual conversation.

Pain and Temptations to Integrity Before God

Pain is not merely the activity of nociceptors telegraphing their injured state to a person's brain. Pain is a signal that the whole organism is in trouble. Pain is a threat to the very integrity of the person as a whole, especially when the pain becomes chronic.

We see the dialogue of integrity being dramatized in Job's encounter with God. Even though both God and Satan have entered into a laboratory experiment together to test the mettle of Job, the Lord says to Satan, "He still holds fast his integrity, although you moved me against him, to destroy him without cause" (Job 2:3). Job's wife chides him after calamities have befallen him, saying, "Do you still hold fast your integrity? Curse God, and die" (Job 2:9). Job

120

tells his counselors that "till I die I will not put away my integrity" (Job 27:5). Job prays, "Let me be weighed in a just balance, and let God know my integrity!" (Job 31:6). He refuses to be torn to pieces by his agony. He intends to keep the wholeness and completeness of his personhood in face-to-face dealings with God. He refuses to accept the assumption of his counselors that his suffering is punishment for sin, or to make a neat bargain with God for its magical removal. To the contrary, Job's expectation of God is consistency, justice, and an affirmation of his, Job's, integrity.

The integrity of people in pain is tested mightily by the persistent pain they suffer. Their own spiritual interpretation of their relationship to God, vis-à-vis their pain state, is an important issue for your conversation with them. If we look at the test of integrity of being as what is meant more profoundly by the biblical teachings about temptation, then temptation becomes something far more deeply significant than the mere transgression of minor moral codes. Temptation becomes the struggle of the whole being to stand and, having stood everything, to stand in the presence of God as one who is faithful to God and to oneself, even when adversity is heaviest. Seen from this angle of vision, what are some of the major temptations of the patient in pain?

The Temptation of Abandonment

Dietrich Bonhoeffer says (p. 98), "This is the decisive factor in the temptation of the Christian, that he is abandoned, abandoned by all his powers—indeed, attacked by them—abandoned by all men, abandoned by God himself. . . . The man is alone in his temptation." The private worlds of people in pain become their nemesis in the feelings of abandonment and isolation that the pain itself engenders. At the same time, self-deception enters, and pain patients hold back a portion of themselves as a private kingdom of control in relation to both God and fellow human beings in the form of pain games. This amounts to preferring the abandonment in a "to-a-certain-extent" sort of way. Yet, as a patient continues to manipulate surrounding people through pain games, these people in turn begin to withdraw all the more. The self-deception creates the very abandonment which the isolation of the pain patient set in motion in the first place. A vicious cycle of abandonment, creating more abandonment, intensifies the temptation to isolation, forsakenness, and self-pity. Subtly the integrity of the patient is eroded.

A paradox is hidden in the feeling of abandonment. It contains in it the positive expectation of companionship and communion both with God and with one's fellow human beings. Your very presence as a pastor contradicts the abandonment the pain patient may feel. If you, a finite, erring human being, are concerned enough to do away with the distance between you and the patient, how much more can a just and loving God? This is especially true in light of your feeling that you are not there merely on your own initiative but as a messenger, a teacher sent from God. You are there to call that person out of isolation, to establish fellowship, to participate in another's suffering. You can say as much to the patient.

The Temptation of Giving Up and Giving In

The temptation inherent in abandonment is related to a second dimension of temptation in the life of the pain patient. This is the proneness to "give up and give in" in the face of intractable and persistent pain. Those who give up and give in to pain cease to believe they can be part of their own destiny. They lose curiosity as to new ways of outwitting and coping with the pain. Their sense of wonder shrivels. Yet within this temptation there is also a paradox. Ordinarily, the pain patient desires absolute and complete relief from pain as a unique right. Physicians and others seeking to provide help are expected to be all-competent and capable of getting perfect results. The pain patient is often unwilling to give up these unrealistic expectations. In pastoral conversation, the perfectionism of the patient can be gently but firmly challenged. If, instead of giving up and giving in totally to the pain, the patient can give up unrealistic expectations for a total cure and give in to accepting, say, a 65 percent relief, the accompanying relaxation and reduction of stress will possibly increase the 65 percent relief from pain to 75 percent.

The Temptation to Play God

However, for patients to make this kind of surrender touches the nerve of another temptation: the temptation to play god in their expectations and demands of others and the temptation to expect others to be little gods also in their perfection. Out of this temptation comes the spiritual call of patients to "join the human race": to accept their own humanity, to affirm the humanity of their physicians and other therapists, and to be more tolerant of their own and others' limitations and frailties. When this happens, their integrity in their own eyes and in relation to other people becomes more vivid. They live with more dignity and humor in the face of the frailty of the human race. In abdicating the need to be little gods themselves, they are more willing to let God be God and to shift sovereignty to God and not to themselves. As the apostle Paul put it, "We have this treasure in earthen vessels, to show that the transcendent power belongs to God and not to us. We are afflicted in every way, but not crushed; perplexed, but not driven to despair; persecuted, but not forsaken; struck down, but not destroyed" (2 Cor. 4:7–8).

The Temptation to Make Pain One's God

Paul Tillich often spoke of the demonic as the absolutizing of a relative reality. Pain very easily becomes absolute in a person's consciousness. For all practical purposes it takes the place of God as the unconditional controlling force in life. Giving up and giving in to pain in effect sets up a pain patient for this inadvertent kind of idolatry. One pain patient came to a moment of truth for himself when he said, "I will be damned to torment if I sit down and worship this constant pain. I will *not* let that happen. There has got to be a bigger center of my life than this, whether the pain goes away or not." He was rebelling against the tyranny of pain. Religious experience is not by any means always conformity; in this man's search for a "bigger center," his spiritual stance was one of rebellion.

The natural aftereffects of letting pain become one's god are legion. A person moves out of the frame of spirit to accept responsibility for the management disciplines suggested in chapter 7. Such disciplines call patients to accept the personal responsibility of being a part of their own therapy for pain. When a person fails to do this, he or she moves into the "blame frame," in which the whole responsibility for the management of pain is projected upon having an adequate supply of painkilling medications, upon physicians who are not obeying the patient's wishes, upon family members who complicate life by being uncooperative, and so on. Then the pain becomes a tool with which to exercise control over all these other people, manipulating them to move at one's command. In other words, a whole Pandora's box of human self-centeredness is opened when pain itself becomes the pain patient's god.

Pastoral Comradeship in the Struggle Against Temptation

Every good pastor is acquainted with the struggle with temptation. He or she may be carrying a steady amount of personal pain. This need not be part of the pastoral conversation in and of itself;

the wisdom of making it so is determined by the length and depth of the acquaintance and relationship a pastor has with a given patient. In many instances, pastors who have known people over a period of years become also known by them in terms of their own personal illnesses. Even though a pastor is free of physical pain, other temptations are real to those who are honest with themselves. Thus, he or she shares with the patient a common ground of fellowship in temptation.

Hebrews sets the tone of the pastor's comradeship with the pain patient in temptation. The Good Shepherd is portrayed as one who is tempted in all points even as we are. We can approach him boldly and find grace to help in the time of need. Similarly, every good pastor can deal gently with a patient in pain or any other suffering person because he or she is beset with weakness also (Hebrews 4:14 to 5:3).

Listening closely to what the patient says about his or her relationship to God and to those to whom the patient relates day by day reveals to the perceptive pastor what the level of temptation is that the person suffers. Carefully following the leads that the person gives enables a pastor to move the conversation from one level of frankness to another. When you measure the courage of the person to face the specifics of temptation, you encourage frank raising of the issue to the extent that the patient's confidence in you is not undermined. The substance of what has already been discussed in this chapter is, when rightly presented, good food for thought for the person to mull over and consider for acceptance. Yet, right of refusal must be given, and the element of comradeship in spiritual struggle must be maintained with genuine considerateness.

Inasmuch as the oldest, most common, and most persistent set of feelings human beings have about pain is that it is punishment, you as a pastor are in the best position to explore these feelings with a given patient. Listening for feelings of being punished for either real or perceived wrongdoing enables you to get at the burdens about which the patient may have no one else with whom to talk. One man said to his pastor that his pain was "all because of my sin." The pastor did not hasten to reassure but simply asked, "What sin?" Then the patient reported having been greedy and frequently working at a factory job three shifts a day in order to make more and more money. Unburdening himself in a voluntary, uncoerced confession enabled this man to find forgiveness, to start reconstructing his way of life, and to take a more active part in the relief of his chronic back pain and arthritis.

The central function of a ministry of confession in the life of any person is to reconcile the person with God through the power of the presence and forgiving grace of Jesus Christ. God ceases to be perceived by the patient as the punishing enemy, the absent Lord, and becomes the present Friend who participates in a responsible way of life for controlling and healing pain.

The Spiritual Transcendence of Pain

One of our functions as pastors is to encourage and instruct persons in the life and practice of prayer and contemplation. The chief end of prayer and contemplation from a Jewish or Christian point of view is adoration and worship of and conversation with God. The relief of pain is certainly one of the petitions a person can make to God. However, that relief in fact is most likely to come as a side effect of the acts of worship rather than as an end result of prayer. The very acts of worship themselves refocus the center of a person's attention; they direct energy away from pain and invest that energy in an intentional fellowship with God; they produce an awareness of the events of time in the largest possible context of the Eternal; and they restore the perspective of a person, turning his or her helplessness into a conscious comradeship with God. The acts of worship remove the sense of isolation and loneliness and replace it with a feeling of belonging to God and being in communion with God.

Pain Disciplines as a Lower Level of Prayer

In the mood and motives of prayer, all the disciplines discussed in the last chapter for managing pain—rest, relaxation, exercise, weight control, the responsible use of medications, avoidance of addiction to alcohol, medications, food, and work—become more than a lonely bootstrap operation of self-discipline and the "exercise of willpower." Each of these acts becomes a lower level of praying to God and bringing life into harmony with the ways God has created us. In fact, none of these disciplines is limited uniquely to people in pain. Each is an affirmation of the intention of God in creation. Each is a commitment of any person who takes seriously the way in which God has created him or her.

The systematic practice of these disciplines is a practical way of presenting the body "as a living sacrifice, holy and acceptable to God, which is your spiritual worship" (Rom. 12:1). It is the offering up of one's being to God. The body in this sense is not merely the physical substance of our humanity but rather our total personality, which is being consecrated to God in any one or all of the disciplines of relaxation, rest, exercise, the careful use of medications, and resistance to addictions to drugs, alcohol, and work. In pastoral instruction about how to pray, you can speak of these as the acting out their prayers. This kind of choreography of pain actually does something constructive about controlling the power that pain has over people. These disciplines are motions of the whole being in prayer to God. They lift people in pain above their pain rather than letting the pain lord its power over them.

The Practice of Prayer in Assessing Priorities

Once people in pain have come to terms with their limitations and accepted the reality of pain as an ongoing process in their life, they can best be instructed to weigh and consider the particular situations that make the pain worse. What kinds of activities contribute to the amount of pain, and what kinds actually bring relief?

In many instances, chronic pain is episodic in its intensity. It comes in sieges that assault the patient from time to time. These times can be charted and identified. The stress events listed in Holmes's stress events scale are some of these times (see The Social Readjustment Rating Scale, p. 135).

By prayerful anticipation, some of these events can be avoided. Others can be spread out over greater lengths of time, rather than having too many of them descend on a person at once. Others can be interrupted with times of rest or diversion. Pastoral conversation with the patient in pain can take the form of prayerful thought about what can be done to redistribute or to avoid stresses. Direct pastoral advice and encouragement are useful, particularly when the stresses a patient endures or faces are not the kind that involve a major life decision.

Many stresses are unnecessary and are actually invited by the stressed individual. One such stress is conflict with other people. If chronic pain patients can make the connection that being upset and angry at other people's behavior will actually increase their amount of pain, you as a pastor can encourage them to cool it when it comes to losing their tempers, getting into verbal duels with people over trivial matters, and letting other people be a "pain" to them, wherever the pain is located! This can be incorporated into a spiritual exercise of deliberately offering up the annoying situation to God in prayer and asking for serenity after the order of the prayer:

God, grant me
The serenity to accept the things I cannot change,
The courage to change the things I can,
And the wisdom to know the difference.
                    —Reinhold Niebuhr, 1892–1971

One characteristic of chronic pain patients in many instances is that they are prone to fight the system. Tilting at windmills over trivial concerns is a product of their irritability. If this can be brought into pastoral conversation as a spiritual issue for prayer for serenity, then the prayer life itself can relieve these patients of "sweating the small stuff," fretting unduly and thereby exacerbating their pain. "A closer walk with God, a calm and heavenly frame," as William Cowper put it in his hymn, is what is genuinely needed. Pastoral encouragement in this direction makes an otherwise agitated person more serene.

The establishment of priorities as to what is really important comes more easily to those who put the events and relationships in which they are involved into the context of prayer, in the perspective of the eternal God. Pain creates a scarcity of energy. Not many things use more energy than fuming over trivial matters about which little or nothing can be done. The wise conservation of energy is of major importance to the pain-ridden person. Isaiah speaks directly to the situation of the people in pain when he says:

Have you not known? Have you not heard?
The LORD is the everlasting God,
    the Creator of the ends of the earth.
He does not faint or grow weary,
    his understanding is unsearchable.
He gives power to the faint,
    and to him who has no might he increases strength.
Even youths shall faint and be weary,
    and young men shall fall exhausted;
but they who wait for the LORD shall renew their strength,
    they shall mount up with wings like eagles,
they shall run and not be weary,
they shall walk and not faint.

                                        (Isaiah 40:28–31)

Giving Thanks for the Simple Gifts for Relief of Pain

The lot of the chronic pain patient is no different from the common lot of humankind. We become so absorbed in our personal discomforts that we neglect to use and give thanks for the simple gifts of life. Some of these are specific aids for the relief of pain. Take, for example, sunshine and other sources of warmth and heat, water (whether it is cold or warm), and things of beauty that capture the attention and renew the spirit. Using, experiencing, and offering thanks for these simplicities of life is one way of spiritually transcending pain.

From ancient times, people in pain have found their way to the sunshine as a way of relief. For a patient to walk outside on a warm, sunshiny day and feel the gift of the sun on the face, the neck, the back is to experience a relaxing of muscle tension and an easing of pain and to feel grateful. To give thanks to God for this relief is to find kinship with those who were so dependent upon the sun that they worshiped it as their god.

Likewise, people for centuries have traveled to bathe in waters that were at least temporarily helpful to their pain states. The interruption of their stresses to make journeys to these places, the company of other pilgrims, and the placebo effect of their expectations of relief all combined to help them, and the water itself was a soothing balm. Little wonder that some of these centers have become shrines of worship as well. However, the modern person in pain often concentrates too much on painkilling medications to find time to appreciate what a warm shower or tub can do to allay the power of pain. To combine this with meditation and thanksgiving for this simple gift enables a person to transcend the power of pain all the more.

Beauty has been mentioned as one of the simple gifts related to pain relief. In a cosmetic culture such as ours, ugliness and pain can easily become synonymous. Particularly is this true of older persons, who associate pain with aging and aging with ugliness. Therefore, grateful concentration on the beauty of a color, a flower, a tree, a rainbow, a landscape, a work of art, or the sounds of music or silence can lift pain patients above the pain they bear. The entry of a child into the room of a pain patient who loves children is more than a distraction for that person. All these are occasions of thanksgiving.

Paul Tillich on one occasion said that the pastor and the church provide a shaping environment to give new meaning to the experiences through which people have to go. You as a pastor have it within your power to bring ultimate and transcending meaning to the life of the patient in pain by focusing the simple gifts into words of prayer.

Mystical Belief, Practice,
and the Spiritual Conquest of Pain

Earlier in this chapter the comment was made that the control of pain could well be one of the "side effects" of sincere prayer before God. This comment represents one of the convictions of persons such as ourselves who are deeply schooled in the Western Christian belief that God is to be worshiped out of devotion and adoration for God's own Lordship in all of life and not as a means of satisfying our desire for pleasure and the avoidance of pain. God participates in our humanity through the complete humanity of Jesus Christ. The teaching of some of the early church fathers of "patripassion-ism"—that God experiences pain—was rejected. Nevertheless, this teaching has now come up for review.

Kazo Kitamori wrote his *Theology of the Pain of God* in 1963. More recently, however, Jürgen Moltmann has drawn on the thinking of Elie Wiesel, the interpreter of the pain of the Jewish people in the holocaust of Nazi Germany. Moltmann perceives God as being intensely involved in the pain of his people without losing his freedom to transcend and exercise justice above and beyond the pain. God is involved in the suffering itself, which is the "situation of God as well as humankind." He quotes Elie Wiesel (pp. 273–274), himself a survivor of Auschwitz:

> "The SS hanged two Jewish men and a youth in front of the whole camp. The men died quickly, but the death throes of the youth lasted for half an hour. 'Where is God? Where is he?' someone asked behind me as the youth still hung in torment in the noose after a long time. I heard the man call again, 'Where is God now?' And I heard a voice in myself answer: 'Where is he? He is here. He is hanging there on the gallows.'"

Moltmann says that for both Jew and Christian any other answer would be blasphemy. "To speak here of a God who could not suffer would make God a demon." He insists that to speak of an indifferent God would condemn us as human beings to indifference. Of the crucifixion and resurrection of Jesus, Moltmann says (pp. 276–277), "No one need dissemble and appear other than he is to perceive the fellowship of the human God with him. Rather he can lay aside all dissembling and sham and become what he truly is in this human God. Furthermore, the crucified God is near to him in the forsaken-ness of every man." We can add that not only is each person thereby enabled to respond to the participation of God in his or her pain, but, by the fellowship of God in Christ with those in pain, each one is endowed with a mission to reach out with empathy to others who are in pain.

The spiritual conquest of pain on Jewish and Christian bases of faith such as expressed by Wiesel and Moltmann has taken a distinctly mystical direction, whereby the suffering of the person in pain is caught up in the larger suffering of God with the whole human race and with the individual in particular. However, the influence of Eastern religions, notably Hinduism and Buddhism, is now being felt in the more recent blendings of Christian beliefs with Eastern practices of meditation.

The ability of Oriental fakirs to walk on coals of fire without being in pain is duplicated by subgroups of Christians in Greece, for example. Beginning every May 21 in Lankadas, Greece, disciplined fire walkers, clutching icons of St. Constantine and St. Helen, dance as much as twenty minutes on flaming logs. Christos Xenakis, a neurologist who has been studying these fire walkers since 1974 under the auspices of the Max Planck Institute in West Germany, searches for the secret of their incredible mastery over pain. He notes that the fire is hot enough to burn, 250–300 degrees Centigrade. Their feet are not covered with thick calluses; only two out of ten even develop blisters. Xenakis feels that there must be some neurophysical explanation (Gage, p. 11).

The villagers say that the saints in whom they believe protect them from the pain, but they have no explanation for how this happens. The mechanism of their miracle remains a mystery to the research team. And the whole process is declared idolatrous and heretical by the bishop of the region.

Mystical beliefs demonstrably have a biochemical effect of some kind either on the pain threshold or on the tolerance level of pain or on both. What these effects are we are only beginning to discover. Let us look at some possibilities.

Hypotheses for Spiritual Anesthesia of Pain

First of all, both Hindu-Buddhist and Christian forms of mystical anesthesia are rooted in centuries of tradition, supported by the wide acceptance of a face-to-face community of believers and richly endowed with unquestioned rituals. The fire walkers in Lankadas may go back to pre-Christian times. Specific origins are traced to the thirteenth century, when the church in Kosti in eastern Thrace (now in Bulgaria) went up in flames, yet villagers who rushed in to save its icons of the saints were untouched by the fire.

Add to this remarkable tradition and community support the fact

that these fire walkers are *not* chronic pain patients. They are deliberately exposing their feet to the noxious stimulus of fire in the
presence of an emotionally inspiring audience. The stimuli are external ones, not internal such as cancer pain, trigeminal neuralgia,
or low back pain. This prompts us to ask whether we are attempting
to compare essentially similar things, or whether we are talking
about two different kinds of pain perceived differently and experienced in radically different settings. In fire walking, the person
is heroic; in chronic pain, the person is a victim. The fire walker
suffers with the massive support, admiration, and affection of the
community; the person in chronic pain suffers in considerable isolation and with doubtful community support or none at all.

Nevertheless, the example of the fire walkers does raise dramati-
cally the need for hypotheses to appreciate, if not to explain fully,
the nature of spiritual anesthesia.

The Placebo

Previous discussion of the placebo effect affirms that what people
in pain believe about surgery, medications, warm baths, exercises,
and the like directly lowers their perception of pain. More recent
research hypothesizes that the confident frame of mind of the patient itself releases the body's own natural opioids to raise the
threshold at which pain is felt. This is yet to be demonstrated at the
laboratory experimental level.

Physiological Changes in Spiritual Meditation

As Edward Thornton says in his book *Being Transformed: An Inner
Way of Spiritual Growth* (p. 57):

> A breakthrough in research came with development of encephalo-
> graphic readings (EEG). Four states of consciousness are linked with
> levels of EEG activity. On a scale from zero to 26 hertz (Hz) per
> second, the EEG measures frequency and intensity of brain wave activ-
> ity.

There are four stages of consciousness and levels of relaxation and
centered attention: Beta (26–12 Hz), or focused attention for rational decision-making; Alpha (12–8 Hz), or defocused attention, a
peaceful, pleasant blankness; Theta (8–4 Hz), or reverie, a half-
conscious dreamlike imagery state; and Delta (4–0 Hz), or sleeping
consciousness. In the experience of pain, Alpha and Theta consciousness seem to provide the most respite from the perceptual

mass of imagery that pain presents in the Beta stage of rational thought.

Spiritual anesthesia can be achieved in biofeedback, in such secular forms of meditation as Transcendental Meditation, or in distinctly Christian forms of meditation and prayer. For a Christian to repeat the words of a given scripture, the name of a biblical character or saint, or simply one word of a valued and cherished belief, such as "Grace," relaxes the whole musculature, shifts the focus of thought away from pain to a restorative rather than upsetting center, and—a side effect of the process—lowers the amount of pain. Herbert Benson, in the book *The Relaxation Response* (pp. 110–111), says that there are four prerequisites for this kind of relaxation: quiet environment; an object, such as the words mentioned above, or a specific symbol, such as a cross, to dwell upon; a passive attitude in which a person empties all thoughts and distractions; and a comfortable posture.

Benson frankly draws upon, but does not restrict his discussion to, the teachings of Christian mystics. He reminds us (p. 115) that

> to prepare for prayers of inward recollections, the true language of the heart, in which one concentrates solely upon God, one must achieve a passive attitude by dwelling upon an object. It is necessary to have the heart free itself and become joyous in order to prevent thoughts from intruding. For the objects upon which one concentrates, Luther suggests the words of the Lord's Prayer, the Ten Commandments, the Psalms, or a number of the sayings of Christ.

Benson suggests two methods of concentration: gazing—that is, fixing one's eyes on the ground, the floor, or a symbolic object— and repeating "no" to distracting thoughts that occur.

Benson suggests practicing this discipline for 20 minutes or more at least twice a day. Whereas he does not relate this to physical pain, we can do so in our context here. What we need to ask is whether this kind of meditative relaxation turned into prayer does indeed create any specific physiological changes that raise either the threshold of pain or the tolerance level to pain, or both.

In chapter 3 we learned about the neurons in the brain and spinal cord that mediate endorphins, which integrate sensory information relating to pain and emotional responses. The field of neurobiology is moving at a fast pace to identify what the painkilling properties of these endorphins are and how they work. It is known that meditation and hypnosis increase endorphins and demonstrable EEG changes in Alpha and Theta states of relaxation. Prayer can do likewise. We know that the relaxation response and inner serenity alleviate pain and its tyranny over the consciousness of a person in pain. It is not unreasonable to move toward further research as to the direct and indirect efficacy of meditation and prayer states in the relief of pain. Already Pelletier in the use of biofeedback has demonstrated (pp. 289–290) that "an abundance of alpha activity appears to help an individual to remove himself from . . . pain and not react to it as intensely. Patients still feel the pain, but it is usually reported as a dull sensation rather than a sharp and throbbing one." The mystics of the Christian faith and of Eastern religions have experienced these results for centuries. We are only now beginning to understand the mechanisms—how these things occur—so that we can repeat the results again and again for the relief of suffering people.

The Anesthesia of a Great Purpose in Life

We have already learned how soldiers at Anzio Beach were made less aware of pain from wounds by reason of their overriding purpose to return home alive. In the same way, football and basketball players caught up in the intention to win a game seem to be oblivious to pain from injuries.

Twenty-three years ago, John Bonica established the University of Washington Medical Center's Clinical Pain Service, which has become a model for pain clinics all over the country. Specialists from eight or ten different specialties combine their efforts to unravel the mysteries of pain syndromes in people who already have "suffered much under many physicians," as the Gospel of Mark (5:26) puts it.

When we learn more of this remarkable man, we discover that he himself lives and moves and has his being in a life of pain. At the age of 67, he says that only his intense involvement in his work keeps him from being "a completely disabled guy" ("Unlocking Pain's Secrets").

Here is a man who like the soldiers and athletes described earlier, is caught up in a purposeful life that lifts him above the tyranny of pain and energizes him to be of service to many other people.

One of the major contributions that you as a pastor can make to people anywhere is to inspire them to a calling and a commitment that overrules and outdistances the thousand mortal ills to which the flesh is heir. Bonica seems to have found this as a direct result of the pain he has to endure. This response to what W. O. Carver called "the glory of God in the Christian calling" is rarely mentioned as an anodyne for pain. Indeed, getting away from pain as a direct object does not do it. The pain itself becomes the life vocation. Rather, as is true of the centered worship of God, the wholehearted pursuit of God's calling seems to have as one of its side effects the assuagement, the relief, and at times the cure of pain.

This book has taken the two of us as authors and you as our reader on a journey of uncharted regions for the pastor to travel. Yet we set out upon the journey through the gateway of the persons' consciousness of physical pain. This gateway for you may be a new one into the spiritual existence of your people. We hope that this book will become a much used "road map" for you as you become, in John Bunyan's words "a 'Mr. or Ms.' Interpreter" and that your church, your study, your home will become to pain-ridden persons a "House of the Interpreter" to guide, comfort, and even heal them of unnecessary pain and to sustain them as they bear the necessary pain in their beings. May you heal sometimes, remedy often, and comfort always in the name of our Lord Jesus Christ.

The Social Readjustment Rating Scale

Life Event	Mean Value
1. Death of spouse	100
2. Divorce	73
3. Marital separation	65
4. Detention in jail or other institution	63
5. Death of a close family member	63
6. Major personal injury or illness	53
7. Marriage	50
8. Being fired at work	47
9. Marital reconciliation	45
10. Retirement from work	45
11. Major change in the health or behavior of a family member	44
12. Pregnancy	40
13. Sexual difficulties	39
14. Gaining a new family member (e.g., through birth, adoption, oldster moving in)	39
15. Major business readjustment (e.g., merger, reorganization, bankruptcy)	39
16. Major change in financial state (a lot worse off or a lot better off than usual)	38
17. Death of a close friend	37
18. Changing to a different line of work	36
19. Major change in the number of arguments with spouse (either a lot more or a lot less than usual regarding child-rearing, personal habits, etc.)	35
20. Taking out a mortgage or loan for a major purchase (e.g., for a home, business)	31
21. Foreclosure on a mortgage or loan	30

Life Event	Mean Value
22. Major change in responsibilities at work (e.g., promotion, demotion, lateral transfer)	29
23. Son or daughter leaving home (e.g., marriage, attending college)	29
24. In-law troubles	29
25. Outstanding personal achievement	28
26. Wife beginning or ceasing work outside the home	26
27. Beginning or ceasing formal schooling	26
28. Major change in living conditions (e.g., building a new home, remodeling, deterioration of home or neighborhood)	25
29. Revision of personal habits (dress, manners, association, etc.)	24
30. Troubles with the boss	23
31. Major change in working hours or conditions	20
32. Change in residence	20
33. Changing to a new school	20
34. Major change in usual type and/or amount of recreation	19
35. Major change in church activities (a lot more or a lot less than usual)	19
36. Major change in social activities (clubs, dancing, movies, visiting, etc.)	18
37. Taking out a mortgage or loan for a lesser purchase (e.g., for a car, TV, freezer)	17
38. Major change in sleeping habits (a lot more or a lot less sleep, or change in part of day when asleep)	16
39. Major change in number of family get-togethers (a lot more or a lot less than usual)	15
40. Major change in eating habits (a lot more or a lot less food intake, or very different meal hours or surroundings)	15
41. Vacation	13
42. Christmas	12
43. Minor violations of the law (e.g., traffic tickets, jaywalking, disturbing the peace)	11

(Reprinted with permission. An earlier version of this table appeared in Thomas H. Holmes, and Richard H. Rahe, "The Social Readjustment Rating Scale," *Journal of Psychosomatic Research* 11:213–218. Copyright 1967, Pergamon Press, Ltd.)

Appendix
of Drug Names

Acetaminophen

Datril	acetaminophen
Excedrin P.M.	acetaminophen
Tylenol	acetaminophen

Anticonvulsants

Depakene	valproate
Dilantin	phenytoin
Tegretol	carbamazepine

Antidepressants

Adapin	doxepin
Asendin	amoxapine
Aventyl	nortriptyline
Desyrel	trazodone
Elavil	amitriptyline
Endep	amitriptyline
Etrafon	perphenazine and amitriptyline
Ludiomil	maprotiline
Marplan	isocarboxazid
Nardil	phenelzine
Norpramin	desipramine
Pamelor	nortriptyline
Parnate	tranylcypromine
Pertofrane	desipramine
Sinequan	doxepin
Surmontil	trimipramine
Tofranil	imipramine

Triavil	perphenazine and amitriptyline
Vivactil	protriptyline

Antimigraine Combination Medications

Axotal	aspirin and butalbital
Bellergal	phenobarbital, ergotamine tartrate, and belladonna alkaloids
Cafergot	ergotamine tartrate and caffeine
Esgic	butalbital, caffeine, and acetaminophen
Fiorinal	butalbital, aspirin, and caffeine
Midrin	isometheptene mucate, dichloralphenazone, and acetaminophen
Wygesic	propoxyphene hydrochloride and acetaminophen

Antimigraine Single Ingredient Medications

Ergomar	ergotamine tartrate
Ergostat	ergotamine tartrate
Gynergen	ergotamine tartrate

Inderal	propranolol hydrochloride	Numorphan	oxymorphone
Nardil	phenelzine sulfate	Percocet	oxycodone and acetaminophen
Periactin	cyproheptadine hydrochloride	Percodan	oxycodone
Phenergan	promethazine hydrochloride	Stadol	butorphanol
		Talwin	pentazocine hydrochloride

Major Tranquilizers (Antipsychotics)

Haldol	haloperidol
Loxitane	loxapine
Moban	molindone
Navane	thiothixine
Prolixin	fluphenazine
Stelazine	trifluoperazine
Thorazine	chlorpromazine
Trilafon	perphenazine

Minor Tranquilizers (Anxiolytics)

Ativan	lorazepam
Centrax	prazepam
Librium	chlordiazepoxide
Tranxene	clorazepate
Valium	diazepam
Xanax	alprazolam

Narcotic or Opiate Derivatives

Codeine	codeine
Darvon	propoxyphene
Demerol	meperidine
Dilaudid	hydro-morphone
Dolophine	methadone
Heroin	diamorphine
Levo-Dromoran	levorphanol
Morphine	morphine sulfate
Nisentil	alphaprodine

Nonsteroidal Anti-inflammatories

Advil	ibuprofen
Butazolidin	phenylbutazone
Clinoril	sulindac
Dolobid	diflunisal
Feldene	piroxicam
Indocin	indomethacin
Meclomen	meclofenamate
Motrin	ibuprofen
Nalfon	fenoprofen calcium
Naprosyn	naproxen
Nuprin	ibuprofen
Rufen	ibuprofen
Tolectin	tolmetin sodium

Salicylates

Anacin	aspirin and caffeine
Ascriptin	aspirin and Maalox
Bayer	aspirin
Bufferin	aspirin
Ecotrin	aspirin
Empirin	aspirin
Excedrin	aspirin, acetaminophen, caffeine

Steroids

Decadron	dexamethasone
Hydrocortisone	hydrocortisone
Kenalog	triamcinolone
Prednisone	prednisone
Solu-Medrol	methyl-prednisilone

Glossary
of Pain-relevant Terms

A-DELTA FIBER   Class of neurons endowed with thick myelin surrounding the axon, which conducts pain signals at a fast rate.

ALGOAGNOSIA   The lack of pain perception in the face of normal sensation.

AMINO ACIDS   Chemicals that are basic building blocks of a protein when assembled in a chainlike series.

ANTALGIC   Referring to the protection of a body area due to pain in that region.

ANTERIOR   *See* VENTRAL.

ANTEROLATERAL SPINOTHALAMIC TRACT   White-matter tract that conducts sensory information from the ipsilateral dorsal horn to the contralateral thalamus.

ANXIOLYTIC MEDICATION   Drug used to alter anxiety by chemically interfering with the limbic system.

AQUEDUCT   Spinal-fluid-filled channel in the brain stem connecting the ventricles with the spinal cord region.

AUTOIMMUNE INFLAMMATORY DISORDER   A class of diseases in which normal protective functions are turned on the body instead of only toward bacteria and viruses.

AXON   Long projection of the neuron responsible for conducting electrochemical impulses away from the cell body toward the synaptic ending.

BRIQUET'S SYNDROME   Psychic disorder of predominantly women manifest by somatic complaints that mimic organic disorders.

139

BROMPTON COCKTAIL   Orally effective mixture of morphine, alcohol, chloroform water, cocaine, major antipsychotic tranquilizer, and flavoring syrup, developed to relieve pain in cancer patients.

CELL BODY   That part of a cell that contains the nucleus and is responsible for carrying out the synthetic functions of the cell; also called soma.

CEREBRAL CORTEX   Thin layer of gray matter on the surface of the brain.

C FIBER   Class of neurons with no myelin covering that conduct pain information at a slow rate.

CONGENITAL INDIFFERENCE TO PAIN   Inborn alteration in the normal perception of painful stimuli as noxious or aversive.

CONTRALATERAL   Referring to the opposite body side.

CORTICOSPINAL TRACT   Fiber tract that carries information from the brain cortex to the ventral horn motor neurons.

DENDRITE   Spindly branch emanating from the cell body of the neuron that receives information from nearby neurons or transduces other changes in the environment via specialized receptors.

DORSAL   Referring to the back of the body (including the spine and buttocks); posterior.

DORSAL COLUMN   Fiber tract on the posterior surface of the spinal cord responsible for pressure and vibration sense conduction.

DORSAL or POSTERIOR HORN   Region of the spinal cord composed of neurons that receive sensory information from the periphery before sending the information to higher levels.

ENDOGENOUS   Originating within the organism.

ENDORPHIN   Endogenously produced brain proteins with opiatelike analgesic qualities.

ENKEPHALIN   A kind of endorphin.

EPICRITIC PAIN   *See* FAST PAIN.

EPIDURAL SPACE   Region just outside the brain and spinal cord, between the dura mater and the walls of the vertebral canal.

EXCITATION Stimulation, either mechanical, electrical, or chemical.

FAST PAIN Sharp pricking pain mediated by the A-delta fiber and the neospinal pathway; epicritic pain.

FEEDBACK INHIBITION System where the product or process generated turns off the production of itself.

5-HT *See* SEROTONIN.

5-HYDROXYTRYPTAMINE *See* SEROTONIN.

GANGLION Collection of many neurons.

GATE THEORY OF PAIN CONTROL Presynaptic blocking of C fiber pain signals in the dorsal horn of the spinal cord by simultaneous stimulation of A-delta fibers.

GRAY MATTER Regions of neuron cell bodies that appear gray when seen with the naked eye.

HYPOTHALAMUS Gland situated just above the pituitary that is responsible for appetite, hormonal regulation of the pituitary, and water retention by the kidneys; called the fight-or-flight gland for its role in the limbic system.

INHIBITION Process of decreasing the probability that a neuron will be electrochemically excited.

IPSILATERAL Referring to the same side of the body.

LIMBIC SYSTEM Interconnected brain regions and structures related to emotion and behavior.

MEDIAL LEMNISCUS Continuation of the dorsal column in the brain stem that relays the dorsal column signal to the thalamus.

METASTASIS Tumor development in a different body part from the region or organ of origin but of the same type of cancer.

MYELIN SHEATH The insulating covering around the axon produced by the Schwann cell.

NALOXONE Man-made drug able to displace other substances from opiate receptors.

NEOSPINAL PATHWAY Referring to the pain signal course from thalamus to the brain sensory cortex responsible for fast pain production.

NEUROLYTIC   Chemical or process that destroys a nerve fiber.

NEURON   Basic cell of the central nervous system that is endowed with electrochemical excitability for communication with other neurons.

NEUROPATHIC   Referring to disorders affecting primarily peripheral nerves.

NEUROTRANSMITTER   Any of a number of specialized chemicals in the central nervous system capable of communicating information between neurons when released at the synapse.

NOCICEPTION   The neuronal signal that denotes pain.

OPERANT CONDITIONING   Behavior conditioned by the response of skeletal muscle response after the presentation of a discriminative cue.

PAIN   The perception of real or threatened tissue damage.

PAIN ASYMBOLIA   Indifference to the perception of pain.

PAIN THRESHOLD   Level of stimulus intensity at which a subject reports pain.

PALEOSPINAL PATHWAY   Referring to the pain signal course from the spinothalamic collateral branches to the brain stem reticular activating system and periaqueductal gray region.

PARESTHESIA   Symptom of pins and needles sensation secondary to altered CNS or DNS function.

PERIAQUEDUCTAL GRAY   Brain-stem region of neurons surrounding the aqueduct that are heavily endowed with serotonin and endorphin receptors.

PITUITARY   Master gland of the body located just under the larger mass of the brain.

POSTERIOR   *See* DORSAL.

POSTSYNAPTIC   Referring to the dendritic side of the synapse.

PRESYNAPTIC   Referring to the axonal end of the neuron where the synapse may be inhibited or stimulated to release neurotransmitters.

PROSTAGLANDINS   Naturally occurring body chemicals that induce pain, inflammation, blood vessel dilation, and fever.

PROTOPATHIC PAIN *See* SLOW PAIN.

RADICULAR BACK PAIN Pain due to the encroachment of a nerve as it exists from the spinal cord.

RECEPTOR Specialized structure upon the neuron surface that causes the cell to be stimulated or altered in its function.

RESPONDENT CONDITIONING Stimulus-paired behavior originally based on reflexive behavior; e.g., salivation.

SCHWANN CELL Specialized cell intimately wrapped around the axon to serve as insulation for electrochemical current conduction.

SEROTONIN Neurotransmitter functionally significant in pain, sleep, and emotion; called also 5-HT, or 5-hydroxytryptamine.

SLOW PAIN Dull burning pain of poor localization mediated by the C fiber and the paleospinal pathway; protopathic pain.

SOMA *See* CELL BODY.

STEREOTACTIC SURGERY Operation performed using a long thin probe placed in the brain under x-ray guidance before an electrical or thermal lesion is produced.

STIMULATION-PRODUCED ANALGESIA Electrical stimulation of the nervous system that renders analgesia beyond cessation of the stimulation.

SUBSTANCE P Naturally occurring chemical in the spinal cord that causes increased pain fiber stimulation.

SYMPATHETIC GANGLION Long strap of ganglions positioned upon the lateral vertebral column which contain cell bodies of the nerves coursing their way from the spinal cord peripheral regions for control of blood vessels and sweat glands.

SYNAPSE Specialized ending of the neuron axon that is responsible for releasing small packets of neurotransmitters which stimulate the next neuron in the pathway.

THALAMUS Structure deep in the brain composed of neurons associated with sensory, emotion, and memory processing.

TRANSCUTANEOUS NERVE STIMULATION Mild electrical stimulation of the skin to reduce pain by spinal cord gating mechanism.

VENTRAL   Referring to the front of the body (including the face and navel); anterior.

VENTRAL or ANTERIOR HORN   Region of the spinal cord composed of neurons responsible for controlling muscles.

VENTRICLE or VENTRICULAR SYSTEM   A hollow spinal-fluid-filled channel in the deep middle of the brain that communicates with the space surrounding the spinal cord.

WHITE MATTER   Regions made up predominantly of axons with pearly white myelin covering.

Bibliography

Arnold, William V. *The Power of Your Perceptions.* Westminster Press, 1984.

Bakan, David. *Disease, Pain and Sacrifice: Toward a Psychology of Suffering.* University of Chicago Press, 1968.

Beecher, H. K. "The Measurement of Pain." *Pharmacological Reviews* 9:190 (1957).

———. "Pain in Men Wounded in Battle." *Bulletin of the U.S. Medical Department* 5:445–454 (1946).

Benson, Herbert, and Miriam Klipper. *The Relaxation Response.* Avon Books, 1976.

Berne, Eric. *Games People Play: The Psychology of Human Relationships.* Grove Press, 1964.

Bok, S. "The Ethics of Giving Placebos." *Scientific American* 231:17–23 (Nov. 1974).

Bonhoeffer, Dietrich. *Creation and Fall: Temptations.* Macmillan Publishing Co., 1971.

Cinciripini, Paul, and Alice Floreen. "An Assessment of Chronic Pain Behavior in a Structured Interview." *Journal of Psychosomatic Research* 27(2):117–123 (1983).

Cousins, Norman. *The Anatomy of an Illness as Perceived by the Patient: Reflections on Healing and Regeneration.* W. W. Norton & Co., 1979.

Davis, Glenn Craig. "Endorphins and Pain." *Psychiatric Clinics of North America* 6(3):478 (Sept. 1983).

Engel, George, and Thomas Szasz. "Psychogenic Pain and the Pain Prone Patient." *American Journal of Medicine* 26(6):900 (June 1959).

Evans, Frederick J. "The Placebo Response in Pain Reduction." *Advances in Neurology,* vol. 4. Raven Press, 1974.

Fairchild, Roy. *Finding Hope Again: A Pastor's Guide to Counseling Depressed Persons.* Harper & Row, 1980.

Fletcher, Carol. "Pain Slowly Surrenders Its Secrets as Research Seeks Safer Opiates, New Class of Analgesics." *Journal of the American Medical Association* 252(23):3236 (Dec. 21, 1984).

Frank, Jerome. *Persuasion and Healing: A Comparative Study of Psychotherapy.* Oxford University Press, 1961.

Freud, Sigmund. "On Narcissism: An Introduction (1914)." *The Standard Edition of the Complete Psychological Works of Sigmund Freud,* vol. XLV (1914–1916). Tr. by James Strachey. London: Hogarth Press, 1957.

Gage, Nicholas. "Greek Ritualists Invoking Saints Walk on Coals." *New York Times,* Sunday, June 1, 1980, Sec. 1, p. 11.

Goddard, Frank A. *The Human Sense,* 2nd ed. John Wiley, 1972.

Jacobson, Edmund. *Anxiety and Tension Control: A Physiologic Approach.* J. B. Lippincott Co., 1964.

Kitamori, Kazo. *Theology of the Pain of God.* John Knox Press, 1963.

Kramlinger, Keith G., et al. "Are Patients with Chronic Pain Depressed?" *American Journal of Psychiatry* 140(6):747–749 (June 1983).

Louisville (Kentucky) *Courier-Journal,* September 16, 1984, p. A3.

Lynch, James J. *The Broken Heart: The Medical Consequences of Loneliness.* Basic Books, 1977.

Marty, Martin. *A Cry of Absence: Reflections for the Winter of the Heart.* Harper & Row, 1983.

Melzack, Ronald. "The McGill Pain Questionnaire: Major Properties and Scoring Methods." *Pain* 1:277–299 (1975).

———. "Psychological Concepts and Methods for the Control of Pain." *Advances in Neurology,* vol. 4. Raven Press, 1974.

———. *The Puzzle of Pain: Revolution in Theory and Treatment.* Basic Books, 1974.

Merskey, H., and F. G. Spear. *Pain: Psychological and Psychiatric Aspects.* London: Bailliere, Tindall & Cassell, 1967.

Moltmann, Jürgen. *The Crucified God.* Harper & Row, 1974.

Mutter, Charles B., and Aaron Karnilow. "Hypnosis: A Viable Option in Chronic Pain Management." *Journal of the Florida Medical Association* 70(12):1097–1098 (Dec. 1983).

Ng, L. K., and John Bonica, eds. *Pain, Discomfort, and Humanitarian Care.* Elsevier North-Holland Biomedical Press, 1980.

Oates, Wayne E. *Your Right to Rest.* Westminster Press, 1984.

Patterson, George W. "The Pastoral Care of Persons in Pain." *Journal of Religion and Aging* 1(1):10 (Fall 1984).

Pelletier, Kenneth R. *Mind as Healer, Mind as Slayer: A Holistic Approach to Preventing Stress Disorders.* Delacorte Press, 1977.

Piaget, Jean. *The Mechanisms of Perception.* Tr. by G. N. Seagrim. Basic Books, 1969.

Restak, Richard. *The Brain.* Bantam Books, 1984.

Seeberg, Reinhold. *Text-Book of the History of Doctrines.* Vol. 1: *History of Doctrines in the Ancient Church.* Tr. by Charles E. Hay. Baker Book House, 1956.

Selye, Hans. *The Stress of Life,* 2nd rev. ed. McGraw-Hill Book Co., 1976.

Silber, Thomas. "Placebo Therapy: The Ethical Dimension." *Journal of the American Medical Association* 249(9):246 (July 20, 1979).

Simonton, Carl. *Getting Well Again: A Step-by-Step Self-Help Guide to Overcoming Cancer for Patients and Their Families.* Jeremy P. Tarcher, 1978.

Soulairac, A. "Stress and Its Effects on Behavior and Pain Perception." In *Emotion and Reproduction,* Part A, ed. by L. Carenza and L. Zichella. Academic Press, 1979.

Steere, David. *Bodily Expressions in Psychotherapy.* Brunner, Mazel, 1983.

Sternbach, Richard. "Psychological Dimensions and Perceptual Analyses, Including Pathologies of Pain." *Handbook of Perception,* vol. 6 B, ed. by Edward C. Carterette and Morton P. Friedman. Academic Press, 1978.

———. "Varieties of Pain Games." *Advances in Neurology,* vol. 4. Raven Press, 1974. Pp. 423–434.

Terrien, Samuel. *The Elusive Presence: The Heart of Biblical Theology.* Harper & Row, 1983.

Thornton, Edward E. *Being Transformed: An Inner Way of Spiritual Growth.* Westminster Press, 1984.

Tillich, Paul. *The Courage to Be.* Yale University Press, 1952.

———. *Systematic Theology,* vol. 3. University of Chicago Press, 1976.

Turk, D. C., and R. D. Kerns. "Conceptual Issues in the Assessment of Clinical Pain." *International Journal of Psychiatry in Medicine* 13(1):60 (1983–84).

"Unlocking Pain's Secrets." *Time* 123(24):58–66 (June 11, 1984).

Vaillant, George. *The Natural History of Alcoholism.* Harvard University Press, 1983.

Walsh, T. Declan. "Antidepressants in Chronic Pain." *Clinical Neuropharmacology* 6:271–295 (1983).

Wetzel, Janice Wood. *The Clinical Handbook of Depression.* Gardner Press, 1984.

Index